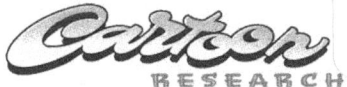

Presents

HAPPY HOOLIGAN

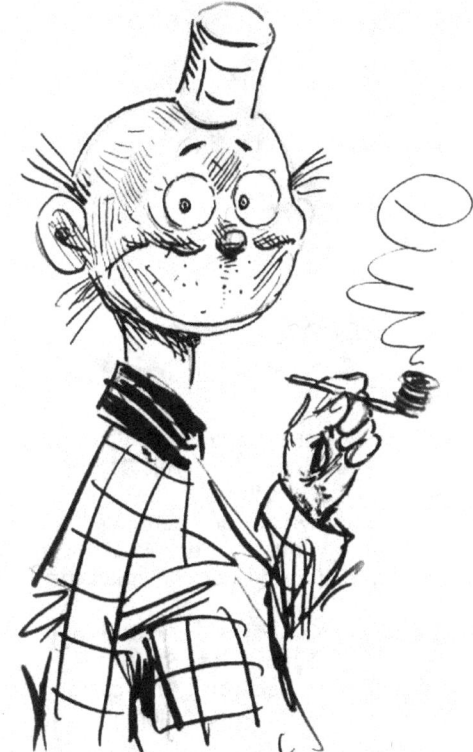

THE ANIMATED CARTOONS 1916-1922

By Kevin Scott Collier

Happy Hooligan
The Animated Cartoons 1916-1922
By Kevin Scott Collier

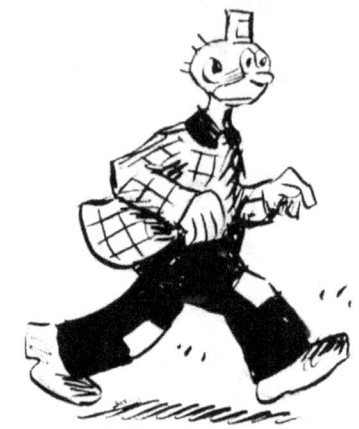

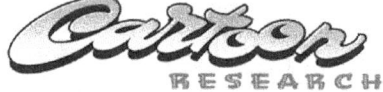
RESEARCH

827 North Hollywood Way #100
Burbank, California 91505
Visit us online:
www.cartoonresearch.com
Founder: Jerry Beck
Email: jerrybeck18@gmail.com

This book is dedicated to
Tommy José Stathes
for his work regarding Bray cartoon film
indexing and preservation.

FOREWORD
The Silent Tramp of Toons

Frederick Burr Opper is best known for his comic creations that he labored over for nearly 60 years of his 80 on Earth.

There are a few books presenting Opper's comics, such as *Happy Hooligan Forever Nuts: Classic Comic Strips*, and *The Early Comics of F. Opper*. He also is mentioned in countless volumes about the history of comic strips.

One thing missing is the story behind his cartoons, and perhaps the word "his" is why they are greatly ignored. He didn't illustrate the animated films, artists like Jack King and Walter Lantz did. Also, the fact that few of the animated films exist today for collectors figures into the scenario. Vintage subjects tend to have a wide fan base in modern times when a celluloid record exists. Imagine the popularity of Charlie Chaplin if only a few of his comedies existed.

At least 55 animated cartoons of *Happy Hooligan* were released from October 9, 1916, to April 23, 1922. Only a small number survive.

The one thing that emerged in research for this book was how wildly popular the cartoons were with audiences. At least until the final year or so. William Randolph Hearst hired the best, most innovative team he could assemble for his International Film Service animation studio. They not only perfected what you saw in terms of motion, but created films that soon would be called "animated comedies," dropping the term "cartoon."

What also emerged during the research was the incredibly brutal pace at which writers, artists and animators were required to work. Many were treated unfairly, and if they survived being fired, they voluntarily resigned.

Animator Bert Green, who worked at International during the *Happy Hooligan* years, stated, "It's no use making any engagements while in this business, as you might as well be serving a sentence in Joliet."

And even with all this, a tramp, who resisted work, and wore an empty tomato can on his head, premiered in theaters to make people laugh.

The record that unfolds is the remarkable stage of early animation, and the importance of story writing in cartoons. They were supposed to be funny, and *Happy Hooligan* was hilarious. During this period of silent cinema, the happy hobo is clearly an animation standout.

- *Kevin Scott Collier*

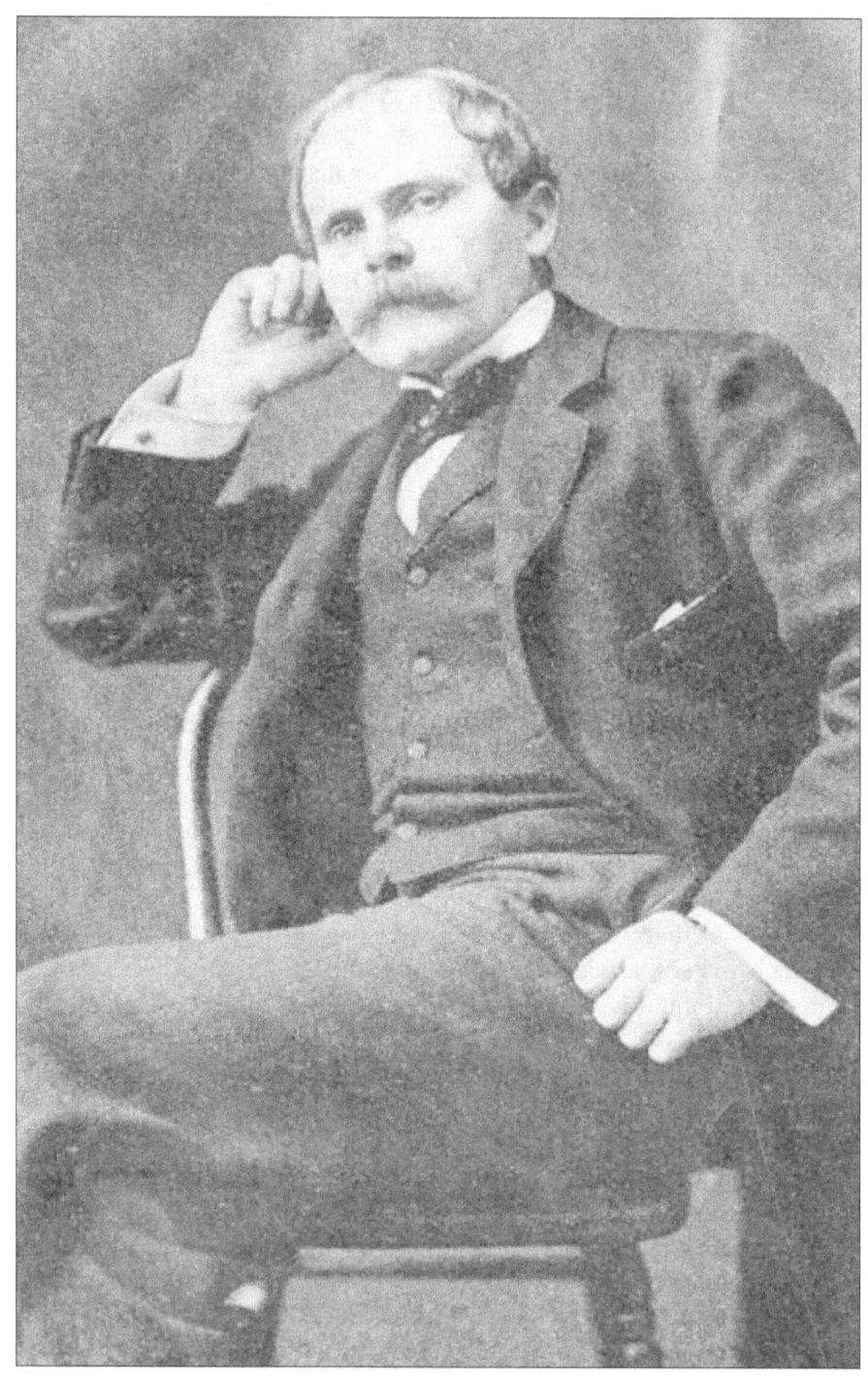

Frederick Burr Opper, as a younger man, sporting a moustache.

CHAPTER ONE
The Pathway to Happy Hooligan

Frederick Burlingame Opper was one of the pioneering character-based comics artists in America. His creations debuting in the pages of William Randolph Hearst's newspapers, *Happy Hooligan* (1900), *Alphonse and Gaston* (1901), and *And Her Name Was Maud* (1904), forever crowned Opper as a king in cartooning history.

A casual poll of cartoonists conducted in the early 1930's produced the result that Frederick Burr Opper was "the funniest man who ever worked for the American press."

Opper, born on January 2, 1857, in Madison, Ohio, was the first of Lewis and Aurelia Burr Opper's three children. His father earned a living in the mercantile business.

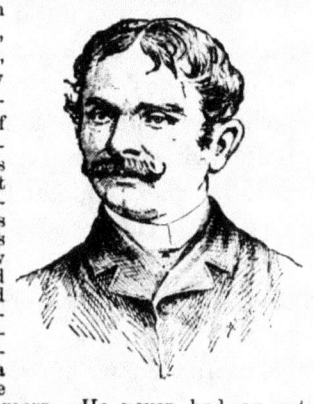

FREDERICK OPPER.

Frederick Opper, probably the funniest of the cartoonists, and the archtype of Hamilton and the other social caricaturists, was born in Madison, Lake county, O., January 2, 1857. Unlike most of his contemporaries, his life is almost barren of incident. His progress has been slow but sure, and he has held but few positions, evidently believing that a rolling-stone gathers no moss. He never had an art education, but drawing seems to have been second nature to him. He drew pictures when at school, and sold many of them to various New York comic papers before removing there in 1875. He also did occasional work for *Wild Oats*, *Harper's Bazar*, and the magazines. In 1877 he joined the staff of Frank Leslie, remaining there three years, at the expiration of which time he went on *Puck*, where he has been ever since.

Frederick Opper mini biography, published in the *Frostburg Mining Journal*, December 17, 1887.

Young Opper dropped out of the public school system at age fourteen, taking a job with a general store, then worked as a printer's apprentice for the *Madison Gazette* newspaper. Two years later, he moved to New York City, finding work as a store clerk. Evenings he practiced his real interest, illustration, by creating amusing drawings.

Frederick Opper was mainly a self-trained talent, with only one term of formal training at New York's Cooper Union. Established in 1858 by philanthropist Peter Cooper, the school offed an education in art, architecture, and engineering.

Opper also gained knowledge of art from working alongside illustrator Frank Beard, as an assistant. Beard's most notable early works appeared in *Comic Monthly*, published from 1859 to 1881. Beard was a respected artist and well-known cartoonist.

Opper submitted cartoons to a variety of humor magazines. His first illustration appeared in the periodical *Wild Oats* in 1876. He subsequently had works published in *Scribner's Magazine* and *St. Nicholas*.

In 1877, he was hired as a staff artist for Frank Leslie's periodicals and magazines. After Leslie's passing in 1880, Joseph Keppler and Adolph Schwarzmann, the publishers of the wildly popular *Puck* magazine, hired Opper, who remained on staff for eighteen years. His duties included covers, story art, and spot illustrations.

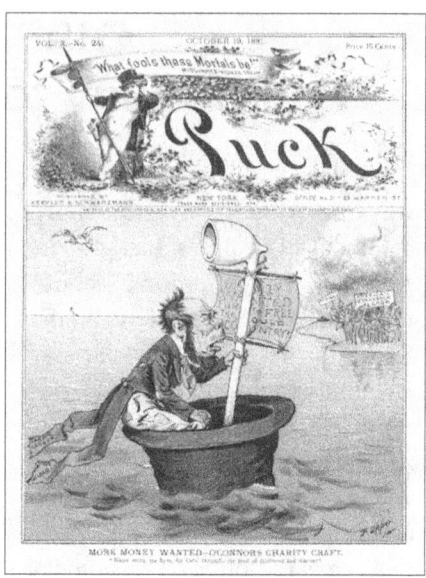

Opper cover for *Puck* magazine, 1881.

Frederick Opper married Nellie Barnett on May 18, 1881. The couple had two children, Lawrence and Sophia.

A syndicated feature story carrying the headline "Noted Cartoonists," published in many newspapers across America in January 1887, named Frederick Opper as one of the lot. The piece presented "a list of artists who are said to influence public opinion."

"The men in New York follow in the path of masters, and contribute to the weekly press [via] our social and political cartoons," it noted.

That same year Opper received praise in the press for being the chief illustrator of Marietta Holley's latest book, *Samantha of Saratoga*.

"The artist's pencil has added rich entertainment," the Democrat Northwest newspaper said, regarding *Saratoga*. "Over a hundred drawings have been made especially to illustrate the text by Frederick Opper, leading artist of *Puck*."

Many newspapers also carried syndicated features highlighting comics artists, which presented short biographies. Opper was one of the cartoonists included in the series.

In 1888, *Puck* magazine published an "Opper Book," presenting a collection of the artist's works. Newspapers announced that the 64-page book, which contained about 360 drawings, was available at most newsstands for 30 cents.

"Nobody can afford to go [to the] seaside or mountains or even out of town for a day, or to stay at home on a hot afternoon without this book companion to while the hours away," the *Washington Critic* reported on June 11.

Frederick Opper's friendly demeanor and humor always made him a favorite personality for the press.

"Frederick Burlingame Opper, the brilliant artist of *Puck*, is a young man, and also a small blonde, who parts his hair in the middle and pokes fun at people in a profitable manner," the *Wichita Daily Eagle* reported on June 22, 1890. "On a pleasant day, when the toil of morning is over, one may meet the evangelical Brunner [Henry Cuyler Bun-

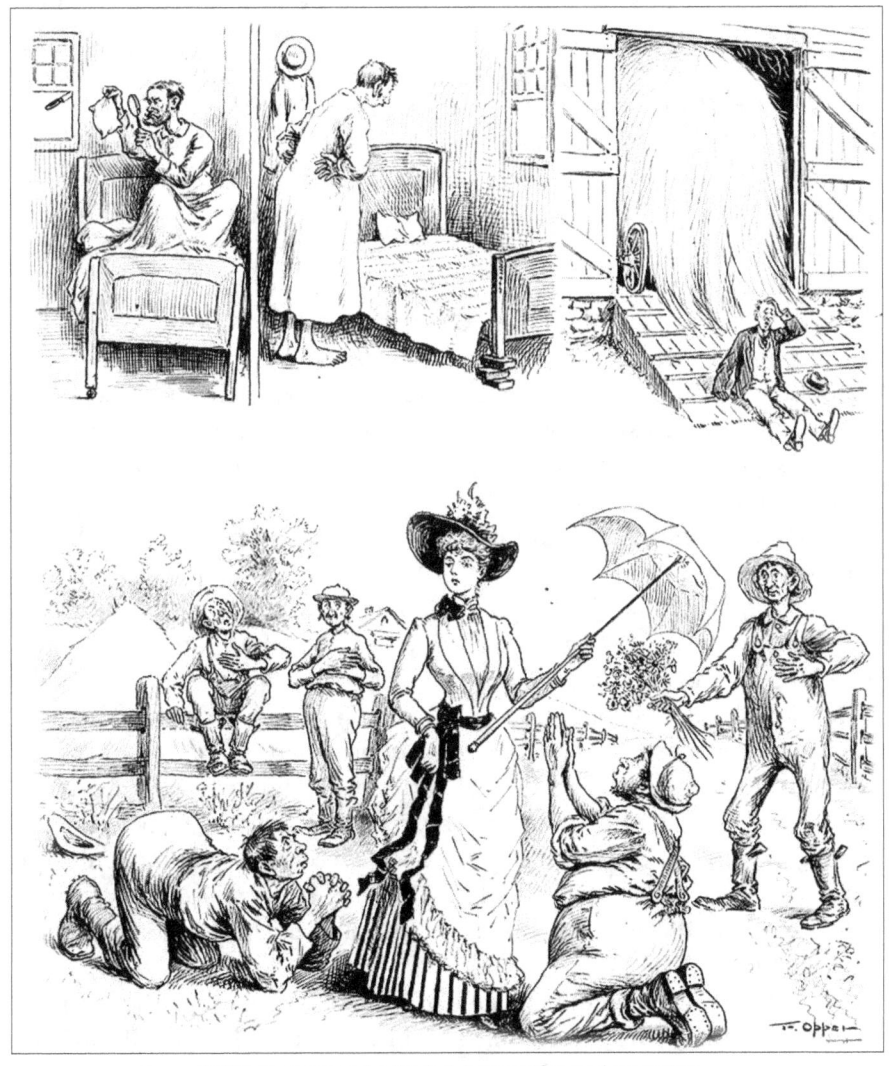

1890's illustrations by Frederick Opper for *Puck* magazine.

7

ner, *Puck* magazine], Opper, and [Charles J.] Taylor at a drug store up near Houston and Broadway [in New York], where they are drinking flavored wind [going for a stroll] and conversing freely with the tradespeople who pass in and out, giving them a pleasant nod of recognition ever and anon."

Frederick Opper's art appeared in several books in the 1890's, often as illustrations to accompany stories. Tales he illustrated for *St. Nicholas* magazine, as well as others, were routinely syndicated to newspapers, where they were republished reaching a wider audience.

Opper's work was virtually everywhere in the 1890's. He often illustrated for humorist writers, such as George V. Hobart, whose syndicated *Dinkelspiel's Conversations*, became a popular syndicated newspaper amusement. Opper also illustrated for noted authors such as Mark Twain and Finley Peter Dunne.

In 1899, the J. B. Lippincott Company published a new edition of *Mother Goose*, illustrated by Frederick Opper. Journalists and entertainment critics praised the book. Frederick Opper talked about the project in a syndicated article.

"While I have kept the tastes of young folks steadfastly in view in making the illustrations for this book, yet the general plan which I have followed might be called, perhaps, the eight-year plan, inasmuch as I have aimed to furnish interest and diversion for anybody up to the age of 80," Opper stated in the article published in *The Indianapolis Journal*, on December 19, 1899.

Opper created 250 illustrations for the book, all presented in black and white.

The cartoonist enjoyed a steady relationship with the J. B. Lippincott publishing company, which also released a successful volume of *Aesop's Fables,* published in 1916, illustrated by Opper.

In 1899 Frederick Opper accepted an offer from William Randolph Hearst to work for his *New York Journal* newspaper. Hearst was establishing a rogues gallery of talented cartoonists and introducing several comics series created by them in his papers. As a result, Opper created *Happy Hooligan*. The character first appeared as a Sunday comic on March 11, 1900. The strip, titled *The Doings of Happy Hooligan*, was syndicated to other Hearst papers, as well, and in short order was published daily.

The comic presented the mishaps of its hobo star, Happy Hooligan. If it weren't for bad luck, Hooligan would have had no luck at all. But, he always remained "happy." The empty tomato can Happy Hooligan wore

THE DOINGS OF HAPPY HOOLIGAN

Yes, it's True! He Wins Out This Time, But His Friend the Cop Catches It by the Bucketful.

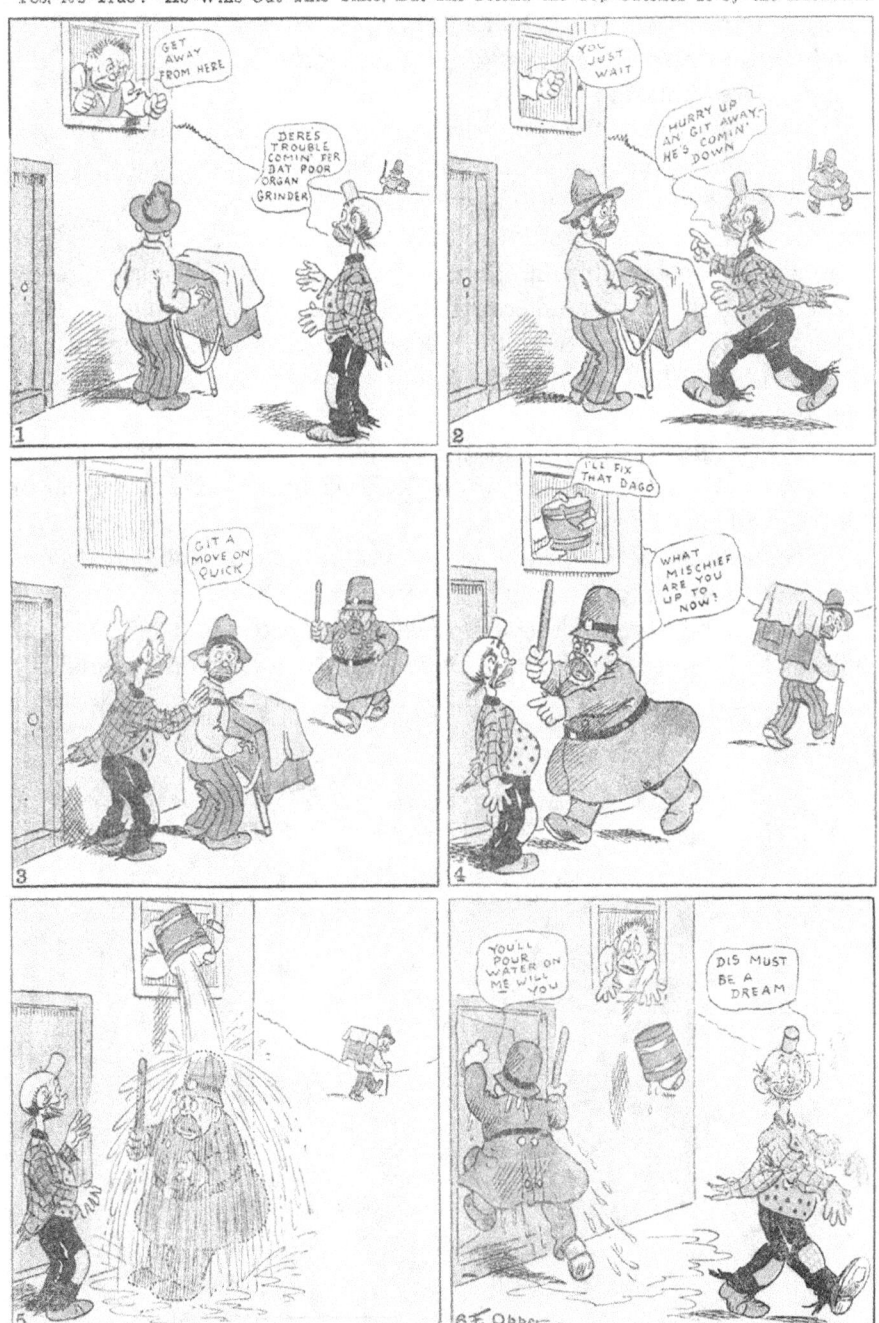

A *Happy Hooligan* comics page published in its first year with Hearst newspapers, 1900.

upon his head became an iconic source of laughter for fans of the funny pages.

Co-starring in the *The Doings of Happy Hooligan* strip, were his brothers sourpuss Gloomy Gus, and Montmorency, a snob. They, like Happy, were bums, too.

"Opper, now one of the *New York Journal's* staff, is among the last of the old school cartoonists, yet few of his admirers would admit that he is any the worse for that," the *Deseret Evening News* reported on October 20, 1900. "His character studies fairly talk from the printed sheet, his tramps are redolent of tramp-dom, and his ward politicians seem ready to step out of the saloon and haul the reader up to straight vote."

In subsequent years, two other Opper comics series, *Alphonse and Gaston*, and *And Her Name Was Maud*, appeared via Hearst newspapers nationwide.

Alphonse and Gaston featured two overly polite Frenchmen. *And Her Name Was Maud* starred a tempestuous mule owned by farmer Si Slocum and his wife, Mirandy.

Opper's success was undeniable, as a syndicated blurb about cartoonists made its way into newspapers in the spring of 1905.

"It pays to be a funny," the *Santa Fe New Mexico* newspaper reported on May 24. "James Swinnertown earns $25,000 a year for drawing silly

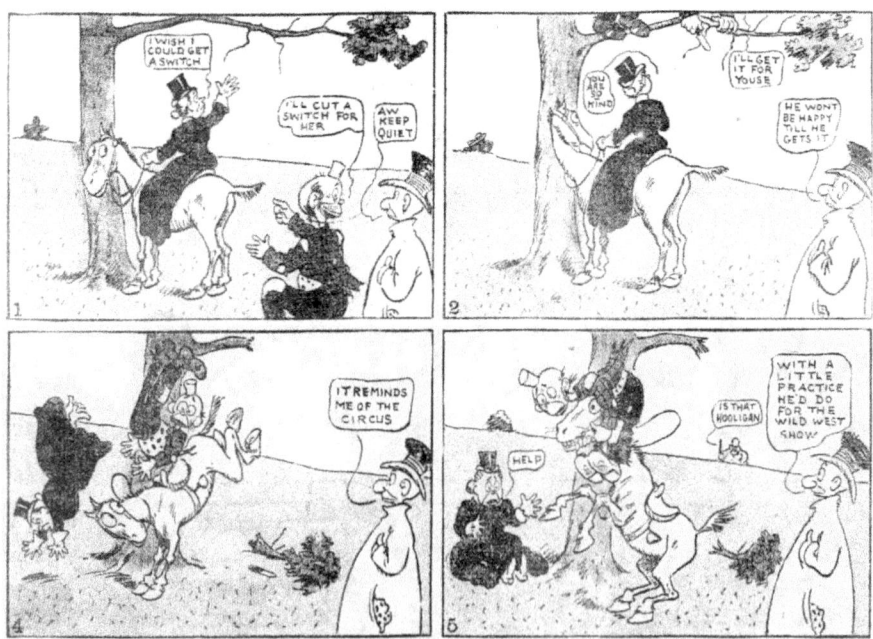

Panels from a *Happy Hooligan* comics strip published August 24, 1902.

10

cartoons; Frederick B. Opper makes a fortune annually drawing *Happy Hooligan* pictures, and [Richard] Outcault comes near making $75,00 a year out of *Buster Brown* and *Yellow Kid* pictures."

The amounts in today's money would put nearly $700,000 in Swinnertown's pocket and over $2 million in Outcault's bank account.

Opper may have not achieved the rank of millionaire, but he had millions of fans because of his three comics titles.

Richard Outcault praised Frederick Opper for his humor in the July 1926 issue of *Circulation*.

"The kind of humor Opper gets into his drawings tickles a certain joint in my risibility that forces a good honest laugh," Outcault stated. "Some comics create in us a gratifying smile on our insides; some please us on account of their ingenuity and good draftsmanship, but Opper's method of expression is purely an appeal to our sense of the ridiculous."

In 1926, *Happy Hooligan* became one of the first comics offered through the King Features Syndicate to gain popularity. Opper retired from illustration in 1934 due to his failing eyesight. Shortly thereafter, on August 28, 1937, Frederick Opper passed away.

There are many excellent books in print about Frederick Burr Opper, his career, and his famous comic strips. But the purpose of this book is to focus on his character *Happy Hooligan* in the context of animated cartoons.

Happy Hooligan made it into motion pictures the same year he made his comics debut, in 1900. But, it wasn't in the form of an animated cartoon.

Next, on the pathway to Happy's animation debut, his live-action comedy shorts.

CHAPTER TWO
The Happy Hooligan Craze

Before comic strip star Happy Hooligan became an animated cartoon in 1916, he headlined a live-action film series starring James Stuart Blackton. Produced by the Edison Manufacturing Company, and shot at the Vitagraph Studios in Brooklyn, New York, *Happy Hooligan* made its celluloid comedy debut in the fall of 1900.

The scenarios and plots for the *Happy Hooligan* comedy films shorts were primarily the invention of Frederick Opper. Blackton, a fan of the comic strip, who developed a close friendship with Opper, was delighted to play a flesh-and-blood rendition of his character.

The first offering in the series, *Hooligan Assists the Magician*, was released in November.

Blackton, who with Albert E. Smith, founded Vitagraph Studios in 1897. He began his career as a newspaper reporter and illustrator employed at the New York Evening World. He was also a cartoonist, caricature artist, and comedy performer, often sharing the stage with Albert Smith. Earning a theatrical reputation as a stage magician, Smith partnered with Blackton, acquiring an Edison Vitascope a year earlier, and the pair became pioneers of early silent entertainment films.

While Blackton played no role in the *Happy Hooligan* cartoon series, which began in 1916, he played a significant role in the development of animation in American film.

At the turn of the 20th century, Blackton would occasion-

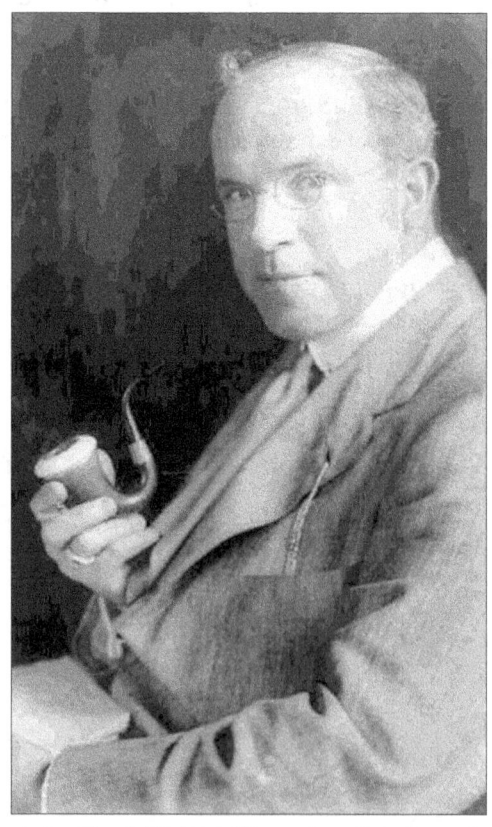

James Stuart Blackton, Vitagraph co-founder, and man who portrayed Happy Hooligan in the live-action film series, 1900-1903.

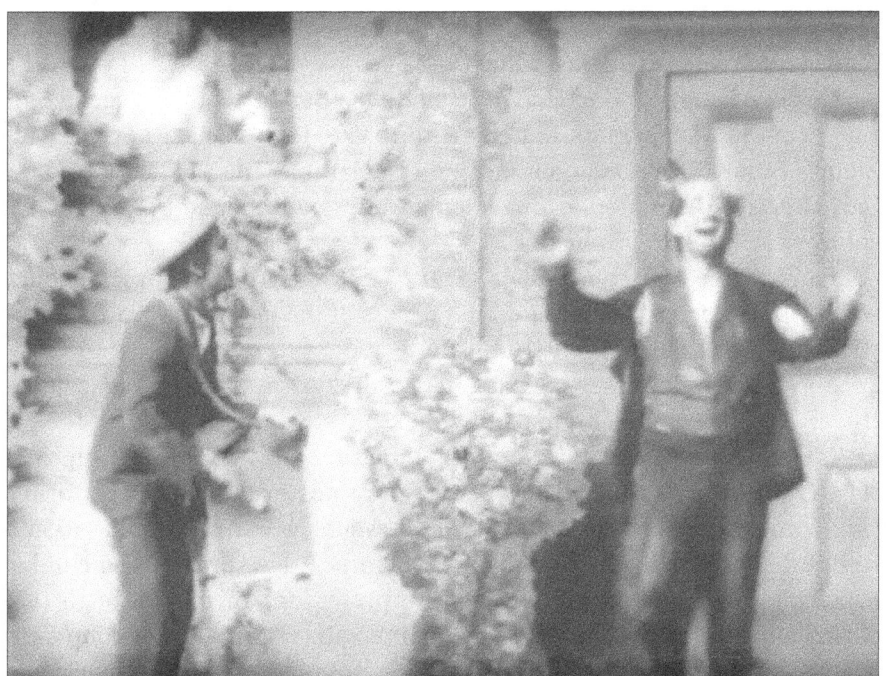

A movie frame from Vitagraph's *Happy Hooligan* live-action film series, shot June 15, 1903. James Stuart Blackman, at right, portrays the comic strip tramp.

ally film himself drawing on a large paper sketchpad and blackboards for theatrical exhibition. His first release, *The Enchanted Drawing*, likely photographed in 1899, depicts Blackton's illustrated performance sketching a face, cigars, and a bottle of wine. It appears Blackton removes the cigars and wine from the drawing, as if they were actual objects. Then, the face momentarily displays an "animated" reaction. The effect, "stop action," was created by stopping the camera, making a single change, then restarting it.

"Stop-motion," which became the standard for film cartoons, emerged in 1905, as the result of an accident. According to Albert Smith, one day while the Vitagraph crew was filming a series of complex stop-action effects, he noticed something upon playing the film back. Smith witnessed in the background a strange effect on steam emitted from the building's generator. He decided to reproduce the intermittent camera exposures deliberately. Subsequently, "stop-motion" was used to create invisible ghosts, or to animate toys as if they were alive.

Blackton used the technique in his film *Humorous Phases of Funny Faces*, released in 1906.

Blackton's love for the emerging presence of comics in newspapers compelled him to look at the funny pages with interest, in bringing a comics character to life in a film.

No sooner had *Happy Hooligan* made his Sunday comics page debut in Hearst newspapers on March 11, 1900, Frederick Opper approached James Stuart Blackton about putting his character into live-action comedy shorts. By summer, arrangements were finalized, and the first of 23 films were put into production.

Vitagraph co-founder, Albert Smith, co-starred in Happy's debut, *Hooligan Assists the Magician*, in the role of the magician, trading antics with Blackton as Happy Hooligan.

An Edison Films press release issued in 1901 provides a synopsis of the *Happy Hooligan* motion picture debut.

"This is a new adventure in which our friend, Mr. Hooligan, appears in an entirely new capacity. On a stage, a professor of magic is performing some wonderful experiments, and when he requests some assistance, Happy Hooligan immediately volunteers his services and climbs upon the platform. As he does so, the professor vanishes through the floor, and the amateur assistant remains with nothing but a couple of barrels, which, however, immediately begin to cut up some remarkable capers. They absolutely refuse to be tampered with, and as fast as Mr. Hooligan knocks them over they regain their balance, and during their evolutions, clowns, ghosts, demons, and goblins appear and disappear in an alarming manner; not, however, without each of them having a crack at the unfortunate Hooligan. Finally he captures two of them, only to find when he yanks them out of the barrels they have changed into immense masses of white muslin, which the professor, who now appears again, divides into two portions, one of which he causes to change into thousands of fluttering bits of paper, while the other at his magic touch forms into a huge and grotesque looking goblin; the whole forming a series of most startling and laughable effects entirely new to animated photography."

While the photography was "animated," the actual cartoon series was off in the distant future. A second live-action *Happy Hooligan* film was released at the end of 1900.

Nine films saw release in 1901: *Happy Hooligan Surprised, Happy Hooligan April-Fooled, Hooligan Visits Central Park, Hooligan Takes His Annual Bath, Hooligan Causes a Sensation, Hooligan at the Seashore, Hooligan and the Summer Girls, Hooligan's Narrow Escape,* and *Happy Hooligan Has Troubles with the Cook.*

According to the *Edison Catalogue, Hooligan Visits Central Park* places Happy on a park bench flirting with two young ladies, who flee. An African-American woman summons a police officer, who chases the hobo out of the park. In *Hooligan Takes His Annual Bath*, two ladies are aghast when they witness the bum bathing fully clothed. The plot in *Hooligan Causes a Sensation* has the bum hard at work sawing wood, while Happy steals the clothing of an ocean bather in *Hooligan at the Seashore*. In *Hooligan and the Summer Girls*, Happy flirts with two farm girls seated in a hammock. Hooligan is almost hit by a train in *Hooligan's Narrow Escape*, and eats a pie cooling on a windowsill and ends up covered in cooking batter and flour.

Edwin S. Porter directed a few of these films; the majority were directed by Blackton and Smith. Porter subsequently went on to make the early cinematic landmark film short *The Great Train Robbery* (1903).

In 1902, a pair of live-action *Happy Hooligan* films saw release, *Happy Hooligan Turns Burglar*, where Happy is accused of grand theft, and *Nothing but Fun*, where he outruns the law after causing an automobile accident.

In 1903, ten *Happy Hooligan* live-action shorts saw release. G. W. Bitzer directed many of these. Among the lot, *Hooligan's Fourth of July* has the hobo getting blown to bits via a firecracker. In *Happy Hooligan Interferes*, the bum encourages a man using an organ-grinder to keep up the noise, which disturbs an elderly lady.

Others entries during the final year of *Happy Hooligan* films have him on roller skates, causing havoc at a summer cottage, working for his lunch, and sharing a Thanksgiving dinner without an invite.

The final live-action *Happy Hooligan* film, *Hooligan's Christmas Dream*, was released in December 1903. The last entries in the series were filmed at the New York studios of American Mutoscope and Biograph Company.

An edition of *The Biography Catalog* provides a synopsis for *Happy Hooligan's Christmas Dream*.

"At the opening of the picture Hooligan is seen wandering about in a heavy snowstorm. He falls asleep in the snow and dreams. In his dreams, he becomes a personage of great wealth and position, with valets and servants to wait upon him. He is reclining luxuriously in a feather bed, and Santa Claus comes down the chimney with pack laden with bottles of champagne, boxes of cigars, etc. Hooligan is soon dressed in the height of fashion and sits to a magnificent dinner. After he has enjoyed this to the utmost, he dreams that he is going to the opera and allows his valet to dress him in his evening clothes. When he attempts to move, however, he finds that his valet has nailed his shoes to the floor. Highly indignant, he starts to chase the valet, but suddenly awakes only to find a big policeman standing over him and rapping his feet with his nightstick. A splendid scene throughout. The Santa Claus scene is omitted when desired, as that portion is appropriate only for the holiday season."

Frederick Opper's comics characters *Alphonse and Gaston* were also the subjects of several live-action Vitagraph short films during this period. The Library of Congress has a small clip from one of the *Happy Hooligan* films, shot on June 15, 1903, in its archives.

Happy Hooligan was also the subject of many civic theater productions around the country, some unauthorized. The most significant was a Broadway Musical, produced by Gus Hill, which took to the stage in 1902. The show, written by Frank Dumont, a former George Christy's Minstrels singer and performer, received positive reviews but was panned by some.

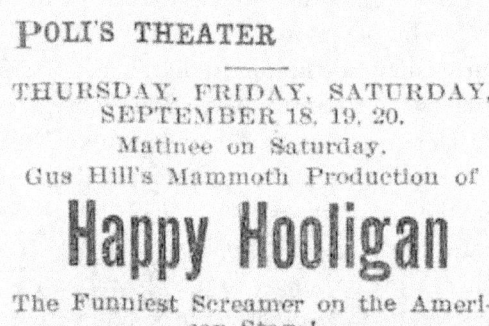

POLI'S THEATER

THURSDAY, FRIDAY, SATURDAY, SEPTEMBER 18, 19, 20.
Matinee on Saturday.
Gus Hill's Mammoth Production of

Happy Hooligan

The Funniest Screamer on the American Stage!

Prices, 25, 35, 50c. Matinee, 25c. Children, 15c. Sale of seats Wednesday, September 11.

A September 19, 1902 newspaper advertisement for Gus Hill's Broadway musical stage production.

"Mr. Dumont, who is accused of writing the piece, did not work hard," the *Indianapolis Journal* reported in its January 10, 1902 edition. "The material is not new. Nevertheless, it was the cause of many a hearty laugh at both performances yesterday."

The play, starring famous vaudeville comedian Ross Snow, unfolded in three acts, featuring a barber shop, trolley car, and courtroom sets. Snow subsequently became a comedic film actor, making his debut in the 1914 Reliance release *The Real Mother*.

Writer J. S. Lawrence trashed the stage play in the *Minneapolis Journal's* December 23, 1902 issue.

"Happy [Hooligan] seems to have escaped the gloom which hangs over this piece bearing his name, the audience is less dexterous and cannot get away from the air of sadness which pervades the production," the *Journal* reported. "Barring the costumes and scenery, what is new is not good and what is good is not new. Frederick Opper should not be held responsible for the dramatizing of his cartoons, for he has contributed nothing to the piece beyond the make-ups of Happy, and his friend, the fat policeman."

Most critics agreed comedian Ross Snow was the only thing good about the show, even though his presence on stage was short.

"Ross Snow in the title role is a success," the *Journal* mentioned. "But he is on stage at infrequent intervals, and he appears only to be hurried away by the cop."

The Gus Hill musical production of *Happy Hooligan* made Opper some money via licensing but primarily was a flop that did damage to the character's funny reputation.

Frederick Opper's *Alphonse and Gaston* also became a stage play touring vaudeville circuits. The production of such ventures was questionable, sometimes bringing Opper criticism, who often had no oversight on licensed projects.

Sometimes advertisers used a *Happy Hooligan* persona in their advertising without authorization. Often, there was little Opper could do. Part of the problem was the artist had named his character after a much-used expression in America describing a joyful hobo, "a happy hooligan." Hamm's Beer was one such example, using the "expression" in their ad, featuring a tramp resembling Frederick Opper's character.

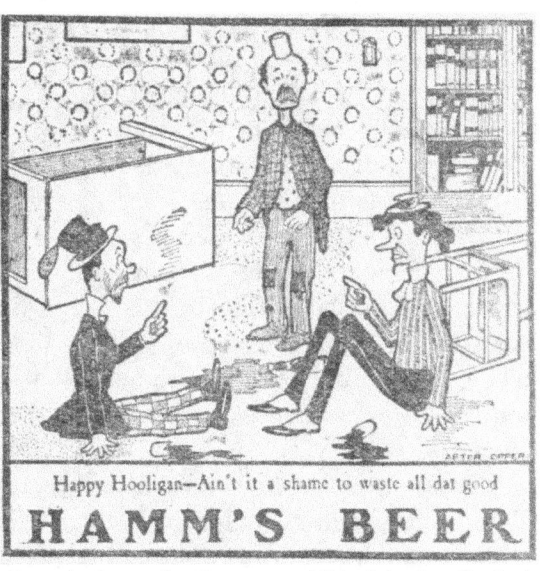

Happy Hooligan—Ain't it a shame to waste all dat good

HAMM'S BEER

Hamm's Beer advertisement published in the St. Paul Globe, April 19, 1902, swiping the Happy Hooligan character. The artist, not Opper, signed the art, "After Opper."

In the fall of 1902, Frederick Opper's name popped up in newspapers across the nation in connection with a check scam. While the report was for the sake of amusement, too many folks were riding on the *Happy Hooligan* wave to the detriment of Opper. The *Akron Daily Democrat*, one of many Ohio newspapers to carry the story, reported the strange incident in its November 17 edition.

"A man claiming to be F. Opper, the New York cartoonist, was arrested Friday on suspicion," the *Daily Democrat* reported. "It is alleged he wrote several checks in a Cleveland bank and attempted to pass them on Barberton merchants. He was poorly dressed."

The police took the man, pretty much dressed "like a hobo," into custody. The suspect had gone into businesses saying, "You don't know me. Gimme a piece of paper, I'll show you who I am. There, that's me, [he wrote] F. Opper. I'm the man who draws Happy Hooligan."

During the period of the *Happy Hooligan* live-action film era, many *Happy Hooligan* fan clubs popped up, not all official through Vitagraph Studios. *Happy Hooligan* costume contests for kids surfaced at schools, outdoor community picnics and festivals, and even in churches. Winners often received prizes at these unsanctioned urban and rural gatherings.

The level of the *Happy Hooligan* craze bordered on overexposure. Fortunately for Opper, fans couldn't get enough of the pitiful tramp.

Subsequently, in 1906, cross-eyed comedic actor Ben Turpin developed a comedy routine titled *Happy Hooligan's Troubles* for Sam T. Jack's Chicago-based vaudeville circuit troupe. Turpin's shtick was tucked within a large company of entertainers presenting a variety of acts. The show toured burlesque houses, circuses and fairs.

Many critics praised Turpin's slapstick act, calling it "a hit."

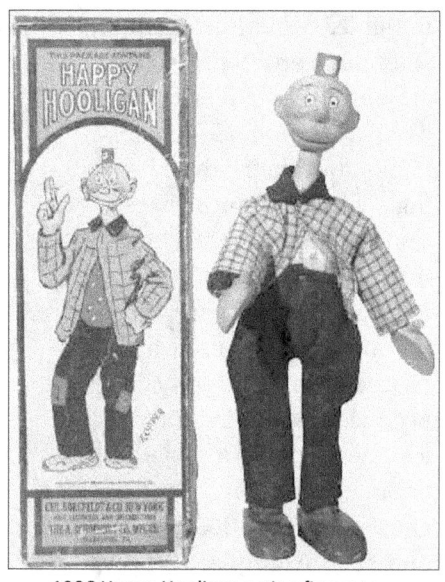

1906 Happy Hooligan action figure toy.

The public never lost interest in Opper's comic strip, even with the barrage of versions and offshoots. Merchandising proved successful, which included games, toys, and an action figure released in 1906.

In 1915, it appeared the character officially resurfaced on film again, but Happy Hooligan's return to celluloid was unauthorized. A lawsuit resulted.

Thus, one year before the *Happy Hooligan* cartoon series made its debut, Frederick Opper was in court battling plagiarism.

CHAPTER THREE
The Bogus Happy Hooligan Film

In the spring of 1914, the Nonpareil Feature Film Company announced it would be producing new live-action films of comic strip favorites. The list included Frederick Opper's *Happy Hooligan*, Bud Fisher's *Mutt and Jeff* and George McManus' *Bringing Up Father*. The first word of the plan surfaced in *Variety*, which conveyed the cartoons were "in active preparation."

The revelation also appeared in the *New York Clipper*, the state's oldest journal of theatrical arts.

"Those screamingly funny character cartoons that have amused millions in the past in the pages of newspapers and on the musical comedy stage as well are to be visualized by the Nonpariel F. F. Co.," the *New York Clipper* reported in its May 9, 1914 edition. "The 'comics' will be single reel offerings, and released at the rate of one a week, the series to run for a year at least."

Nonpariel, operated by William J. Counihan, was producing a film version of *Alice in Wonderland* at the time. The company featured Gus Hill on its payroll as a producer.

Hill, who had licensed the character Happy Hooligan for the production of the 1902-1903 Broadway play, and claimed possession of Frank Dumont's script for the musical, apparently believed he had the right to parse out segments of the play for use in a Hooligan on film.

Counihan hired Jack Mahoney to direct the *Happy Hooligan* series, and comedic burlesque actor Billie Ritchie to play the character. Ritchie had perfected a tramp persona a decade before Charlie Chaplin

Majestic Theatre
COUNIHAN & SHANNON, Proprietor's and Managers
FORMERLY PROCTOR'S

Special | PHOTO PLAY ATTRACTION | "Happy Hooligan" | A BRAND NEW SIDE-SPLITTING COMEDY IN TWO PARTS. JUST RELEASED.

MATINEE AT 2 P. M. EVENING AT 7 AND 9 P. M.

PRICES---Matinee, 5 and 10c. Evening, 5, 10, 15 and 25c.

COMPLETE CHANGE OF SHOW MONDAYS AND THURSDAYS

Advertisement in the Perth Amboy Evening News, New Jersey, August 28, 1914, for the exhibition of the Nonpariel Feature Film Company's unauthorized *Happy Hooligan* motion picture.

19

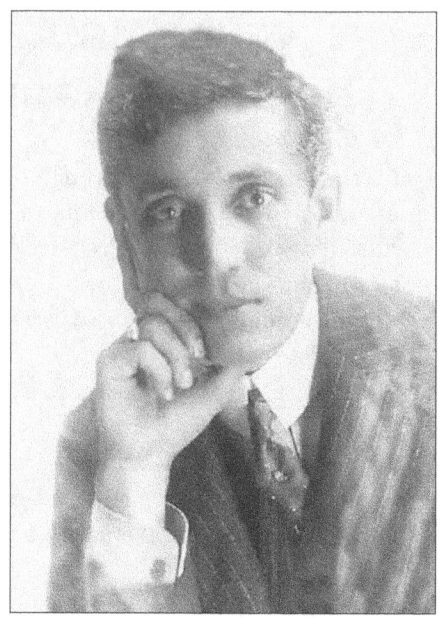

Left, Variety announcement of Gus Hill's *Happy Hooligan*, January 16, 1915. Right, comedic actor Billie Ritchie, was cast in the role of the character Happy Hooligan.

appeared in his first film, *The Tramp*, in 1915, making it his persona. In fact, Ritchie had loaned Chaplin his tramp outfit that he wore in the landmark film. Ritchie and he had become close friends while touring during their vaudeville days. Their troupe had also included pre-film comedian Stan Laurel.

Nonpariel brought in writer Paul Arlington to create story adaptations from the *Happy Hooligan* comic strip—indicating the film series wouldn't just adhere to the Broadway play. The company announced that shooting of their first *Happy Hooligan* film would begin on June 1, 1914.

Nonpariel released the comedy, titled *Happy Hooligan at a Vaudeville Show*, in August that year. Reported as "a comedy feature in two-parts," the film mainly received theatrical bookings in eastern and Midwest theaters.

Nonpariel announced the second film began production in January 1915, *Happy Hooligan at the Seashore*. Vitagraph had previously used the title for a 1901 live-action short.

That fall Nonpariel's run of *Happy Hooligan* came to a crashing end when a copyright infringement lawsuit was filed in New York by William Randolph Hearst's The Star Company. The suit also represented the intellectual property interests of its cartoonist, Frederick Opper.

To sue in New York State, the location of their headquarters, Star claimed Nonpariel had exhibited the bogus *Happy Hooligan* film on October 15 at the Park Row Theater in Manhattan, New York. *Moving Picture World,* using a headline, *Happy Hooligan in Court,* outlined the suit in an article. New York newspapers, chiefly owned by Hearst, publicized the action. They openly attacked Nonpariel for use of the character without expressed permission.

"Suit has been filed in the United States District Court by The Star Company against the Nonpareil Feature Film Corporations, of 1482 Broadway, setting up an infringement of the copyright to the cartoons and character of Happy Hooligan," *Moving Picture World* reported on November 27, 1915. "The Star company, a successor to the *New York Journal* and *Evening Journal,* shows it exhibits of cartoons and its acquirement of the rights to them in all methods of publication."

The published reports noted that Nonpariel could not use the Gus Hill musical stage play beyond its expressed intention and original contract limitations. Motion picture versions based on parts of the play were considered illegitimate.

"The bill says that the defendant company [Nonpariel] commenced the display of a photoplay of this noted picture series at the Park Row theater October 15, last," *Moving Picture World* said. "The bill sets up that the photoplay is built around the Hooligan series designed and created by Frederick Opper and of which the plaintiff owns the copyright. It is alleged that the defendant's play could not have been constructed from any other design and that the plaintiff's rights have been invaded."

The suit did not seek monetary punitive damages, but rather seizure of any profits or income Nonpariel had received from the movie, plus the destruction of the bogus film.

"The prayer [of the defendant] is for injunction, forfeits of all reels, negatives, etc., and an accounting," *Motion Picture World* continued. "Judge Charles M. Hough issued an order to the defendant to show cause on Nov. 26, why an injunction should not be issued."

Nonpariel did not challenge the suit, and shortly thereafter, the company went bankrupt.

Apparently, the judgment did result in the confiscation and destruction of the bogus *Happy Hooligan* films, as none are known to survive.

Moving into 1916, Frederick Opper was presented with an opportunity to return Happy Hooligan to film and restore the character's legitimacy. But it wouldn't be live-action this time. Happy Hooligan would be resurrected in the form of an animated cartoon.

CHAPTER FOUR
Happy Hooligan's Cartoon Debut

Happy Hooligan's leap from the comic's page into the world of animation began with the establishment of William Randolph Hearst's International Film Service. Hearst's notion was to produce short cartoon films based on popular comic strips created by cartoonists on his payroll. In mid-December 1915, the IFS animation studio became operational at 729 Seventh Street, New York. IFS joined dozens of film offices functioning within the same building at the time.

As part of a branch of his International News Service wire, Hearst planned to add cartoons at the end of weekly newsreels and travel films, all exhibited in theaters nationwide. On October 29 that year, Hearst partnered with Brooklyn-based Vitagraph Studios to produce and distribute his newsreels, replacing the Selig Polyscope Company.

Raoul Barre worked as a director of the first cartoons released by the International Film Service. Hearst replaced Barre with Gregory La Cava in January 1916, appointing him supervisor of the operation. Frank Moser joined La Cava's team as chief animator. Other additions included William Nolan, director of animation, Edward A. MacManus, general manager and Clement S. Parsons, chief camera operator.

At the time, aside from owning nine major city newspapers, William Randolph Hearst syndicated comics created by his cartoonists to 500 other papers, reaching over 20 million readers daily. To guarantee the best results for his animation studio, Hearst lured animators from existing studios by offering them twice their pay.

The first nine cartoons produced by the studio featured the creations

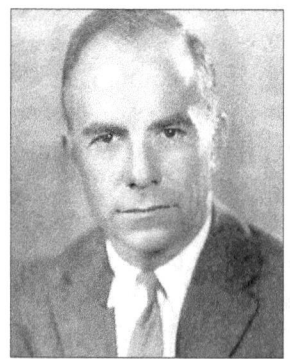 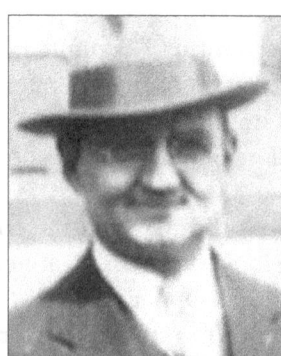 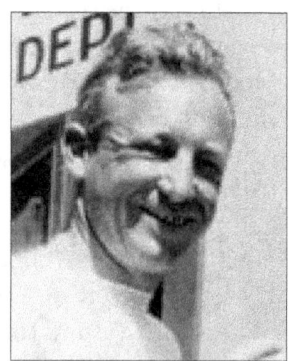

Left to right, International Film Service supervisor, Gregory La Cava, chief animator, Frank Moser and director of animation, William Nolan.

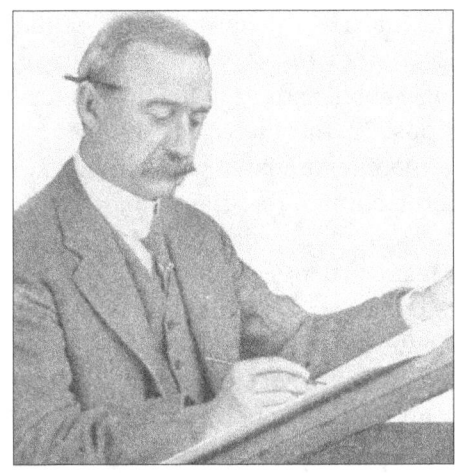

Cartoonist Tom E. Powers.

of Thomas E. Powers, a popular Hearst cartoonist. Powers' first IFS offering, *Feet is Feet*, was released on December 31, 1915. Powers' *Joys and Glooms*, featuring two elf-like characters recognized in his editorial cartoons, also became animation subjects.

George Herriman's first *Krazy Kat* cartoon, *Introducing Krazy Kat and Ignatz Mouse*, was released on Feb. 18, 1916. Artists Bill Nolan and Leon Searle illustrated the series.

These first animated releases carried the Hearst-Vitagraph banner.

Midway into the year, William Randolph Hearst disassociated business operations with Vitagraph. Henceforth, productions carried only the International Film Service branding.

Disappointed in Vitagraph's inability to achieve financial success for his company, Hearst began exploring the viability of establishing his own film exchange company.

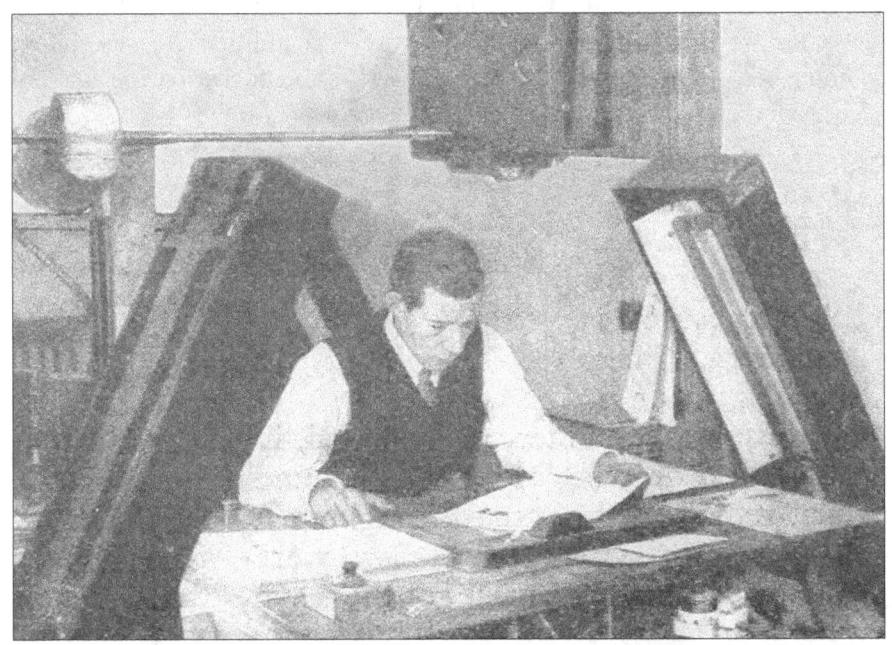

International Film Service's cameraman Clement S. Parsons at work.

International Film Service general manager Edward A. MacManus announced in the April 6 edition of *Motion Picture News* that a chain of exchanges across the nation was being established to handle their entertainment and feature film productions. In the piece, MacManus explained the company's strong commitment to animated productions.

"At this point, I may say we are of the opinion that the animated cartoon is capable of as many variations as any other kind of pictures, and we are going to have the pick of the Hearst artists, cartoonists, and illustrators," MacManus said. "We will make dramas of a different sort, and we are going to attempt not to get into the rut of doing over old ideas."

Frederick Opper was paired with Louis De Lorme to write the stories for the IFS *Happy Hooligan* series and other Opper creations. Artist Jack King was assigned to illustrate the *Happy Hooligan* cartoons.

Subsequently, King worked for several animation studios, including Disney and Warner Brothers. At Warner, he produced the *Merry Melodies* and *Looney Tunes* series. During King's long career, he worked alongside animation icons Tex Avery, Friz Freleng and Bob Clampett.

Louis De Lorme had previously been director of the Victorgraph Film Company, and appeared in several movies as an actor, most notably, *The Clutches of the Loan Shark* (1912).

De Lorme was also a savvy businessman, snatching up a large library of educational films when the General Film Company went out of business, and reselling them for a small fortune. In addition, he was an accomplished photographer. In 1917, Hearst assigned De Lorme to film the second inauguration of President Woodrow Wilson.

Prior to the debut of *Happy Hooligan*, Opper's character Maud the

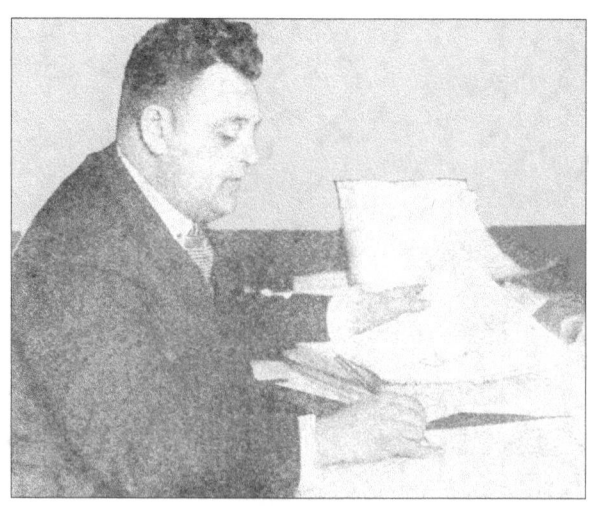
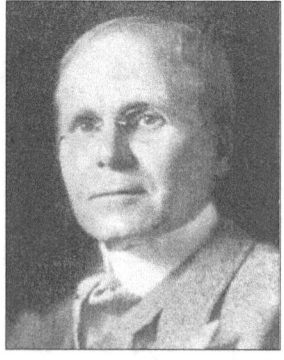

Left, Louis De Lorme works on scripts at his IFS office desk. De Lorme, paired with Frederick Opper, above, wrote the *Happy Hooligan*

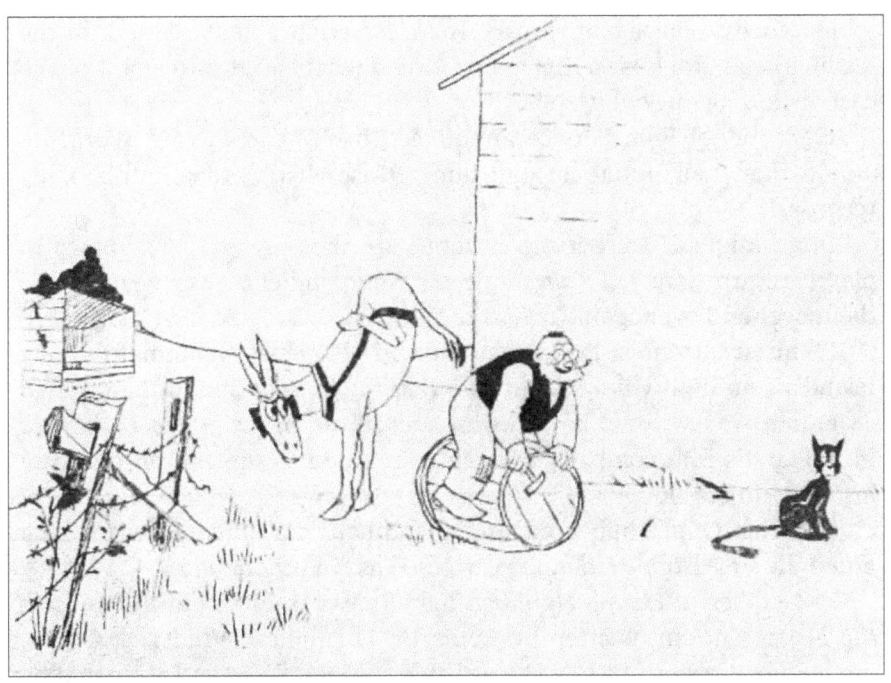

A frame from Frederick Opper's *Maud the Educated Mule*, released July 3, 1916.

Mule, star of his *And Her Name Was Maud* comic, appeared in four animated shorts.

The first Maud cartoon, *Poor Si Keeler*, was released on February 4. In the story, farmer Keeler, who routinely gets kicked by Maud, becomes a traffic cop.

Maud's debut was followed by followed by Opper's *A Quiet Day in the Country*, on June 4, *Maud the Educated Mule,* on July 3, and *Round and Round Again*, on October 2.

Opper's *Maud* cartoons received praise in the pages of entertainment periodicals. *Motion Picture News* recognized one *Maud* cartoon in its July 1 edition, describing the storyline.

"The squire is holding his savings in his hand preparatory to giving them to his nephew when Maud puts her head in the window and gobbles them up," the magazine reported. "Maud gets a slam in the eye and retaliates by kicking the squire across the lots where he strikes a fence wire and bounces back to Maud, who kicks again. Back and forth from wire to hoof goes the squire and there are laughs galore."

On the same day, *Moving Picture World* published a glowing preview of *Maud the Educated Mule*, released two days later.

"*Maud the Educated Mule* is a particularly happy subject for cartoon comedy," magazine wrote. "There is action aplenty. Maud, in the leading heavy role, kicks the everlasting daylights out of the rest of the cast, including our old friend Si."

International Film Service announced in *Moving Picture World* on July 8 that their initial cartoon film releases had "broken all booking records."

"International Film Service cartoons are the only cartoons known to play a return date," IFS announced. "Your audience will want to see them over and over again."

IFS hired cartoonist Bert Green the end of June as an animator. Long Island's community newspaper *The Bay Bugle*, reported in their July 8 issue that Green would be "drawing pictures of *Bringing Up Father* for Mr. Hearst's film company." Green commuted to the IFS offices from his home in Bayside.

Frederick Opper appeared in the company's announcement, which noted the first *Happy Hooligan* cartoon was "in production."

On October 9, *Happy Hooligan* made his cartoon debut in *He Tries the Movies Again*, written by Louis De Lorme and Frederick Opper, directed by Gregory La Cava, illustrated by Jack King, and animated by Frank Mosher.

The title of the animated film short, *He Tries the Movies Again*, was a dismissive jab at Nonpareil's unauthorized film released in 1914. This

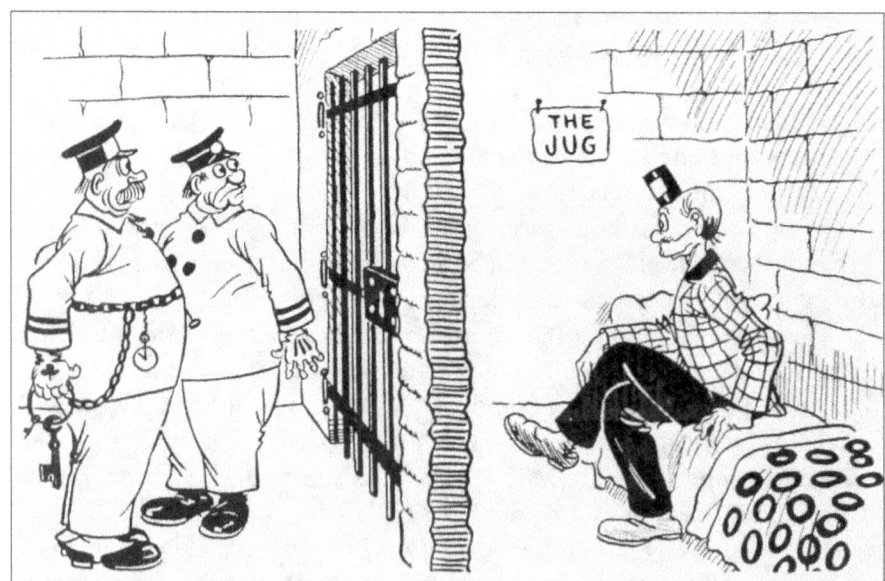

Illustration from the first Frederick Opper *Happy Hooligan* cartoon, *He Tries the Movies Again*, released October 9, 1916.

cartoon *was* Hooligan's *real* return to film.

The cartoon shared a split reel with a Curtis Scenic piece, *The World's Wonderland*, featuring spectacular landmarks in Yellowstone National Park, Wyoming.

He Tries the Movies Again was exhibited as an attraction to feature films, such as *Her Double Life*, starring Theda Bara and Franklyn Hanna, *God's Half Acre*, starring Mabel Taliaferro and Jack W. Johnston,

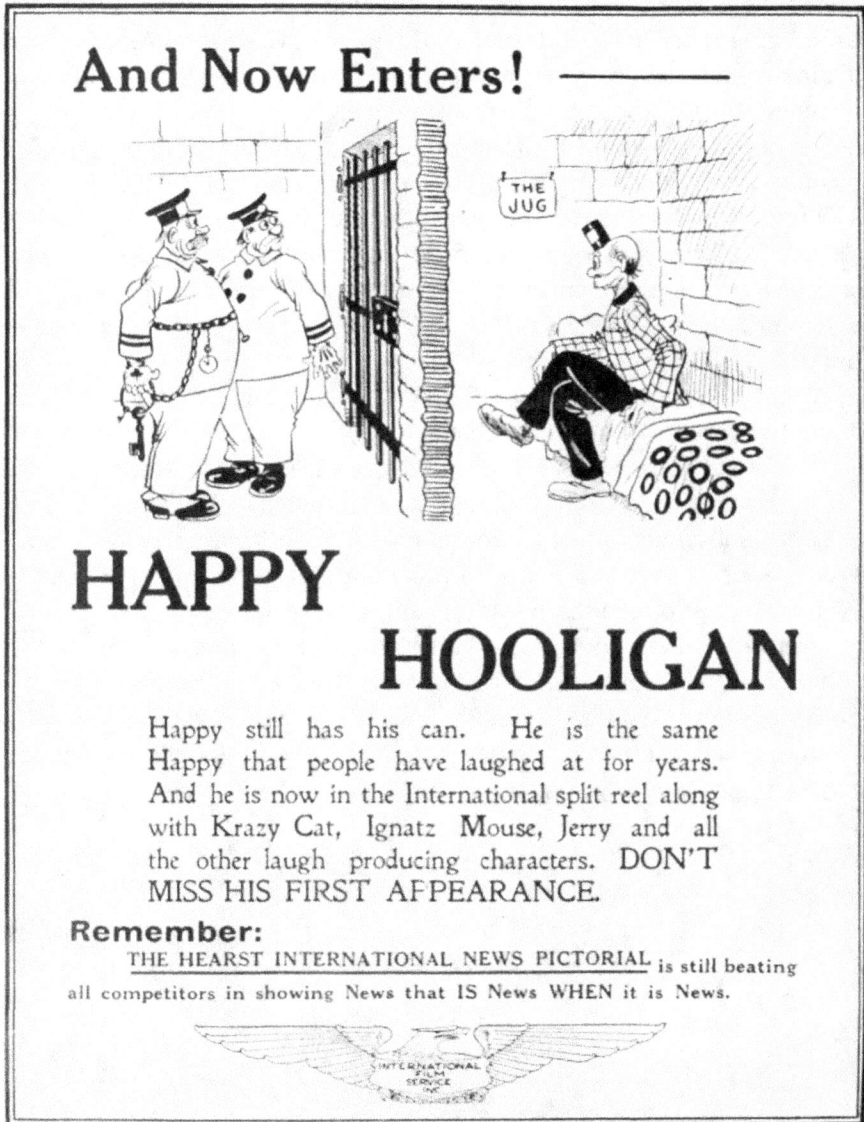

A full-page ad announcing the cartoon debut of *Happy Hooligan,* published in several magazines.

and *Isis*, starring Billie Burke.

The cartoons were part of a Hearst-Vitagraph package, which included Heart's popular newsreels, travel and nature films, and occasionally, a *Hearst Fashion Service* reel.

Most theaters promoted the addition of a *Happy Hooligan* cartoon to their motion picture listings in newspaper advertisements. Occasionally, an ads stated a bonus attraction was simply "a Hearst cartoon."

Also in October 1916, International Film Service, had transitioned from being a branch of International News Service into a separate and distinctive full-service entertainment and feature production entity. This included a syndication and distribution operation.

Hearst hired William H. Johnson as general manager to oversee IFS business operations, with Samuel S. Paquin as assistant.

International Film Service expanded its staff in the fall, adding Vernon Stallings as an animation director, and artist Herbert E. Hancock as an animation manager. William Powers, brother of Tom E. Powers, joined the team as an animator. Tom would leave IFS at the end of the year.

Walter Lantz was hired by IFS that fall and assigned to illustrate an animated version of Walter Hoban's *Jerry on the Job* comic strip. The series debut, *Jerry Ships a Circus*, was released on November 13. The cartoon was co-directed by Stallings and animated by William Powers.

Lantz subsequently went on to create such characters as *Woody Woodpecker*, *Chilly Willy*, and *Andy Panda,* and the establishment of Walter Lantz Productions, a leading animation studio.

International continued to add talent over subsequent months, and its completed team is impressive historically. It included leading cartoonist Foster M. Follett, Isidore Klein, Ben Sharpsteen and Burt Gillett.

Among his many accomplishments, Isidore Klein gained recognition

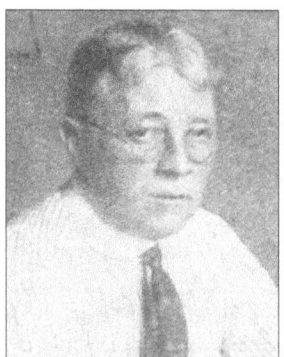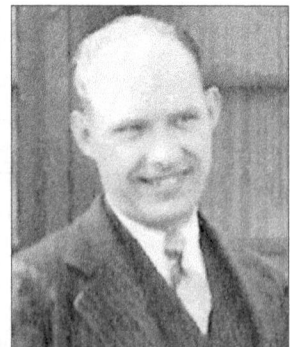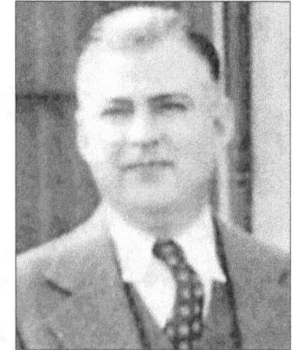

Left to right, International Film Service artists Foster M. Follett, Burt Gillett, and Jack King.

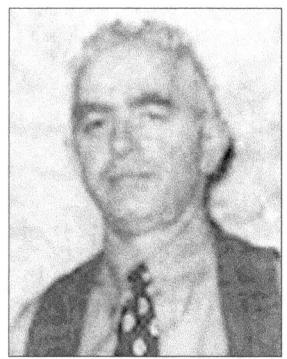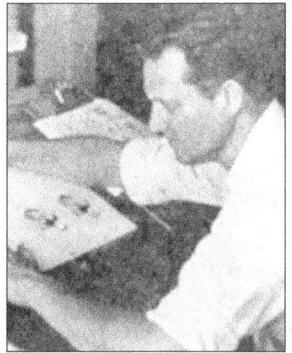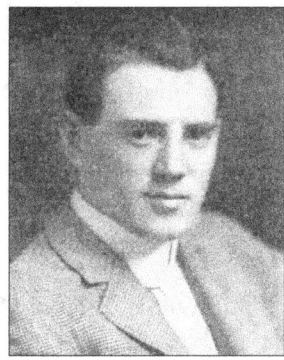

Left to right, International Film Service artists Isidore Klein, Grim Natwick, and Bert Green.

for his *Mighty Mouse* cartoons for Paul Terry Studios. Ben Sharpsteen earned critical acclaim for his work with Disney, particularly on the films *Pinocchio* and *Dumbo*. Burt Gillett subsequently earned fame for his *Silly Symphonies* work for Disney Studios. Foster M. Follett went on to work for John R. Bray as an animator, most notably working on the *Quacky Doodles* cartoon series.

George McManus' *Bringing Up Father*, illustrated by Edward Grinham, made its animated debut on November 21. Grinham, supervised by Frank Moser and Bert Green, had been hired onto the IFS team specifically for this cartoon. Green also assisted with the illustrations.

That fall, IFS began production to introduce Rudolph Dirks and Harold H. Knerr's *The Katzenjammer Kids* into the world of animation. The first cartoon saw release by year's end, illustrated by another addition to the IFS animation department, John Foster.

Artist Grim Natwick was recruited by Gregory La Cava to temporarily fill an animation position until an experienced talent could be secured. His first assignment was a horse race sequence in a *Happy Hooligan* cartoon. William Randolph Hearst was so impressed with Natwick's work, he offered him $100 per week to remain on staff.

Grim Natwick subsequently became recognized for illustrating Max Fleischer Studio's animated *Betty Boop* character.

Unable to establish a viable Hearst film exchange for the distribution of International News Service and International Film Service productions, William Randolph Hearst entered negotiations with Pathé Exchange, Incorporated, the end of the year. In short order, an agreement was signed and an allegiance established.

The year 1916 closed with only one *Happy Hooligan* animated film in circulation. It remained an orphan for several months after its release. The second in the series would see release on February 11, 1917.

CHAPTER FIVE
1917 Happy Hooligan Cartoons

International Film Service's first significant achievement of 1917 was its alliance with Pathé Exchange, Inc. The company maintained offices at 25 West 45th Street, New York. Hearst, before associating with Vitagraph, had used Pathé for the distribution of his early newsreels.

The Hearst-Pathé arrangement officially launched on January 10, and allowed for the distribution of the entire combined film output of International News Service and International Film Service, which produced the series of animated cartoons.

Hearst-Pathé announcement published in *Moving Picture World*, January 13, 1917.

IFS added to its staff animator Gil Martin, and appointed Edgar B. Hatrick as the general manager of photography for the animation department.

It wasn't until on February 11, 1917, that International Film Service released the second *Happy Hooligan* cartoon, *Ananias Has Nothing on Hooligan*. The animation short was tacked at the end of a split reel, featuring "Blackfeet Indians," in a travelogue featuring Glacier National Park.

The plot of *Ananias Has Nothing on Hooligan* centered around antics at The Ananias Club, an establishment boasting a grand membership of tramps and hobos. But once the members see Happy, they realize their hoboism pales by comparison.

The next *Happy Hooligan* cartoon, *Double-Cross Nurse*, released on March 25, tagged along at the end of a split-reel educational film, *Rope Making in Mexico*.

In the cartoon, Happy Hooligan finds a job posing as a nurse, which leads to unpleasant, disastrous results for the patient.

The next, *Happy Hooligan* in *The New Recruit*, observed America's entry into World War I. The cartoon, written, illustrated and animated

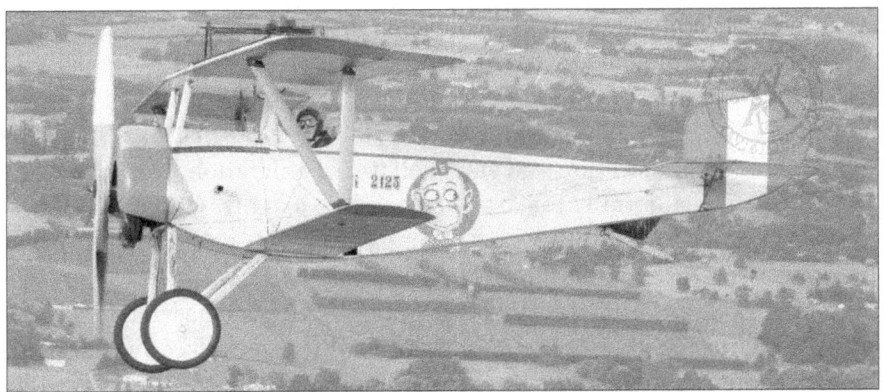
A replica of Alvaro Leonardi's *Happy Hooligan* World War I airplane, reconstructed in 1962.

at lightning speed, was released on April 26, only 20 days after the United States Congress issued a declaration of war on the German empire.

In the cartoon, Happy Hooligan is spinning tall tales to his three nephews about becoming a war hero, after dodging enemy shells to deliver an important message to a general. The children don't buy it, and conclude Happy should be "shot at sunrise" for telling such outlandish falsehoods.

The adventure marked the character's patriotic public relations move in participating in the war effort.

The PR moved did not go unnoticed. Italian flying ace, Alvaro Leonardi, customized his N11 warplane with the colors and image of Happy Hooligan. Today, a replica of the aircraft hangs on display at the San Diego air and space museum.

Moving Picture World reported on April 28 that Pathé Exchange, Inc. "breaks records" in earnings, and the company issued bonuses to its employees. Income from International Film Service's cartoons was part of this success. Frederick Opper earned a mention in the piece.

Happy Hooligan in *Three Strikes You're Out*, released on May 6, placed the character at bat in a major league baseball game. Previewing the cartoon, *Motion Picture World* commented in its May 5 edition, "With baseball season starting, this cartoon is timely."

On May 12, *Moving Picture World* called *Three Strikes You're Out* "a very amusing *Happy Hooligan* baseball cartoon."

The June issue of *Photo-Play Magazine* provided an exposé on animation that allowed a look inside of International Film Service's world of cartoon production.

"Nearly half of the most successful newspaper comic strips have been animated," *Photo-Play* writer Arthur Gavin, Jr., conveyed. "Take, for example, the animated cartoon department of the International Film Service, where the comics that appear in the Hearst and other papers are brought to life."

Gavin went on to explain the inner-workings of International's operation, including illustration and early cell use in animation.

"In an office adjoining the artists' workshop sits Mr. Herbert E. Hancock, the managing director, as we might call him, and also chief scenario writer, working out plots for *Krazy Kat*, *The Katzenjammer Kids*, *Happy Hooligan*, and the other characters. When the scenario is finished, it is turned over to the animator who has specialized in that particular character. Each animator works at a drawing board, in the center of which is a sheet of ground glass, lighted from beneath. The animator is himself a director.

"His actors are the characters originated by the artists who draw them for the newspapers, but who have nothing to do with the work of filming them. The animator, having read the scenario, is ready to begin the first scene.

"Suppose, for example, the story is to start by having *Krazy Kat* come out of his house, about to go shopping. The first thing to do is to draw the setting—the house, trees, a lamp-post, the cobblestones of the street, and the like. These details and all the incidental comedy touches are left to the imagination of the animator. Why we call him the direc-

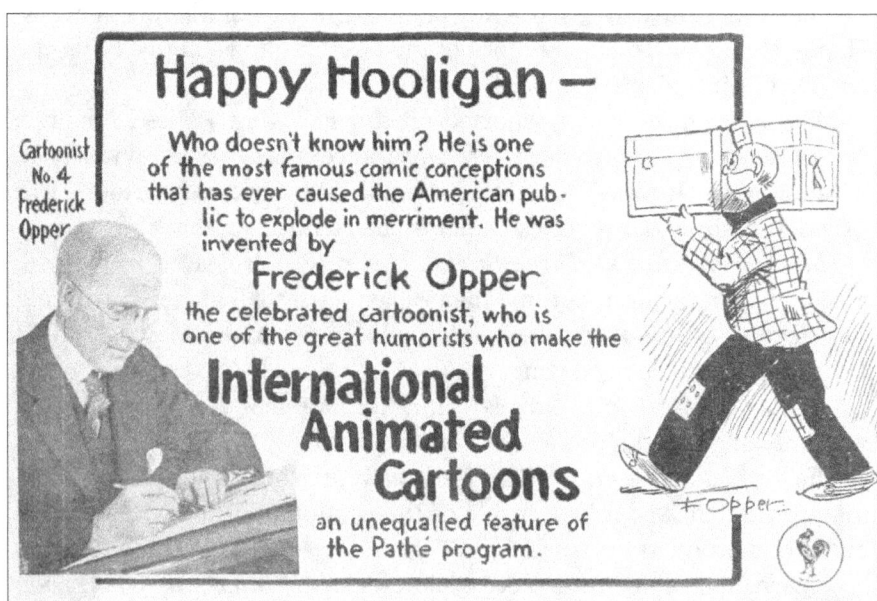

A half-page ad, published in several magazines, July 1917, presenting a profile of Frederick Opper.

tor, is because he builds up the scenario just as a photoplay director does.

"Having drawn his setting on celluloid, he is ready now to put his actors into motion.

"On a sheet of paper he sketches, in pencil, *Krazy's* face, so placed that when photographed together with the setting it will just peep out of the door.

"On a second sheet, *Krazy's* body is sketched, to appear to be just stepping out of the house. Sketch after sketch is made, until the cat has done everything called for in that scene.

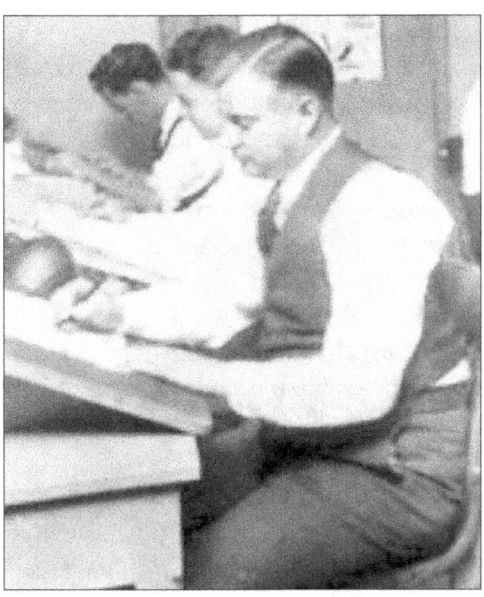

Jack King, who illustrated the *Happy Hooligan* cartoons, seen in this circa 1930 photo, when working for Disney Studios.

"Then, while he goes on with his work, his finished pencil sketches are turned over to members of the staff of tracers and blackers—less-skilled artists who go over the pencil lines in ink and paint in the solid blacks, where indicated by cross marks. This relieves the high-priced director of much of the drudgery, for his time is valuable, and even with all the labor-saving devices that have been invented it takes him a month to complete a single five-hundred-foot film.

"After all the work is done, the great mass of drawings are collected and turned over to the cameraman, who, by referring to the schedule which the animator keeps as he works—and which looks as long and complicated as a railway timetable—is able to figure out how all these parts of pictures are to be fitted together to be photographed.

"This is another slow, laborious process, for the drawings have to be pieced together and changed for each exposure. It requires at least a year to become a proficient animator, and only a man who has had training and experience as a comic artist or cartoonist can hope to qualify for the position," Gavin concludes, in the article.

On June 1, the sixth *Happy Hooligan* cartoon, *The Great Offensive*, was released. The short was tacked on the end of an educational film about training police horses. The July 14 edition of *Moving Picture World* called *Happy Hooligan's* return to the frontlines in the war cartoon, "an excellent one."

International released the next *Happy Hooligan* cartoon, *Around the World in Half an Hour*, on June 10. The whimsical travelogue tale places Happy in a hot air balloon, in a parody of Jules Verne's *Around the World in 80 Days*.

Happy Hooligan in *White Hope*, was released August 8. *Moving Picture World* stated the cartoon was "chock full of laughs." The story places the hobo in a boxing ring, sparring with his opponent in a bout for the title.

"*Happy Hooligan*, the *White Hope*, is one of the best Opper ever did," the magazine said. "The prize fight is a scream and, furthermore, it is one that will pass the censors. An amusing cartoon, *Happy Hooligan*, is the hero!"

The following *Happy Hooligan* cartoon, *Happy Gets the Razoo*, released on September 2, brings the hobo and his brother Gloomy Gus to a primitive island where cannibals reside. The objective of the siblings is to stay off the native menu, and out of their large cooking pot. "It is quite funny," *Moving Picture World* stated on September 15.

Happy Hooligan in *In the Zoo*, was released September 9. In the story, the tramp finds himself inside of the safety of fences facing a caged, hungry, snarling lion.

Happy Hooligan in *The Tank*, released on September 16, presents a patriotic, wartime theme. Happy Hooligan constructs a tank in his barn, equipped with a trench digger. "I'm going to present this to my country," Hooligan tells his brother, Gloomy Gus.

"It depicts in animated drawings the adventures of *Happy Hooligan*, with a fearful and wonderful new invention for war," *Moving Picture World* reported on September 29. "Though, the action is not sanguinary." The magazine, not wishing to be a spoiler, did not reveal Happy's secret weapon was an armored tank.

Happy Hooligan in *Soft*, was released on October 7. In the story, Happy takes a job as an assistant to an invalid, thinking it will be easy. He has second thoughts when his employer puts him through a very active and challenging day.

"In *Soft*, some funny situations arise, and the comic is successful," *Moving Picture World* stated on October 27.

"Happy Hooligan discovers what a really busy life can be led by an invalid with a mania for exercise," *Motion Picture News* reported on October 20. "Happy decides there are easier jobs than attending to such a human dynamo."

The next *Happy Hooligan*, *The Tale of a Fish*, was released on October 16. This time Happy went fishing with a crew of pirates aboard their ship and is taken out to sea. As a result of an argument, the pirates toss Hooligan overboard and an enormous whale swallows him. Lucky for the hobo, he knows the whale, and it spits him out safely on land. The press compared the plot to the tale of Jonah.

"It's a fresh episode in the career of *Happy Hooligan*, pictured in animated drawings, in a tale like Jonah and the whale, amusing and laughable," *Moving Picture World* said, on November 10.

"Happy as a fisherman was once guilty of an act of kindness to a little fish, and apparently fishes have memories," *Motion Picture News* reported on November 10. "So when Happy and the crew of the pirate ship had a difference of opinion, and Happy found himself in the watery depths and about to emulate Jonah, he reaped the reward of his past performance. The cartoon is more than a little funny."

Also released on October 16, was *Happy Hooligan* in *At The Picnic*, Happy, his nephews, and brother, Gloomy Gus, go to a picnic where they encounter some amusing predicaments, including hungry ants. *Moving Picture World* stated on November 3 the cartoon was "a fun adventure," featuring "enjoyable animated drawings."

Another *Happy Hooligan* cartoon premiered on October 16, *At the Circus*. Happy Hooligan and his nephews find entertainment under the big top. There are plenty of animals to see, but one ends up being too close for comfort when the hobo finds himself in the lion's den confronting the king of the jungle.

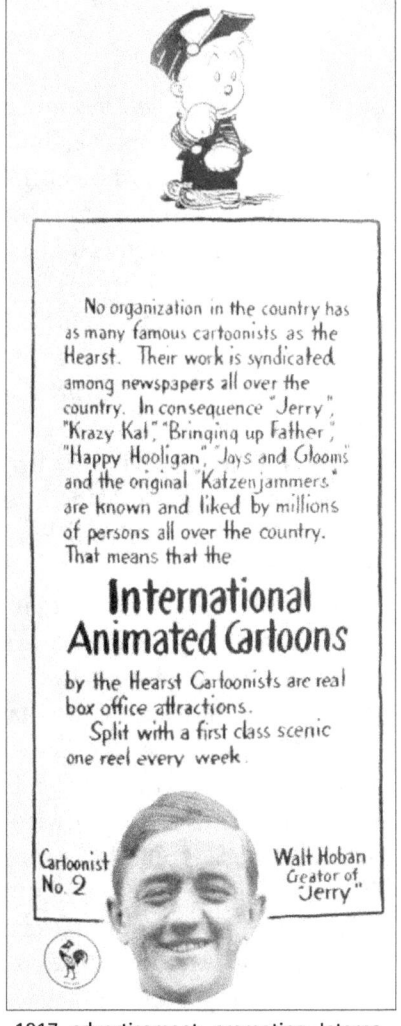

No organization in the country has as many famous cartoonists as the Hearst. Their work is syndicated among newspapers all over the country. In consequence "Jerry", "Krazy Kat", "Bringing up Father", "Happy Hooligan", "Joys and Glooms" and the original "Katzenjammers" are known and liked by millions of persons all over the country. That means that the

International Animated Cartoons

by the Hearst Cartoonists are real box office attractions.
Split with a first class scenic one reel every week.

Cartoonist No. 2

Walt Hoban Creator of "Jerry"

1917 advertisement promoting International Film Service cartoons. Pictured, cartoonist Walter Hoban.

"Happy has an adventure in the lion's den, in an amusing way," *Moving Picture World* reported on December 22.

"Happy Hooligan is featured in a thrilling drama with a startling denouement in At the Circus," *Motion Picture News* said in its December 22 issue.

Happy Hooligan, The Tale of a Monkey, was released November 25. In the story, Happy Hooligan explains to his nephews why they always must be kind to animals. However, his patience is tested by a large, overactive monkey.

"His experiences with the big monkey are very laughable," *Moving Picture World* reported on December 8. "A fine comic."

Bullets and Bull, the next *Happy Hooligan* cartoon, and final release of 1917, appeared on December 8. No animals are harmed in this one. Happy Hooligan shoots the bull, meaning that he exaggerates by telling tall tales. It's others who get the idea of grabbing hold of a shotgun and putting the "bull" out of *their* misery. *Motion Picture News* called it "an extremely funny Happy Hooligan film."

An article in *Motion Picture News*, published on December 8, announced optimistic plans for International Film Service in 1918.

"For the past two years, the International Film Service Company, Inc., which controls the cartoons of all the comic artists of the chain of Hearst newspapers, has been striving for bigger and better animated cartoons," the magazine reported. "With such subjects as *The Katzenjammer Kids, Happy Hooligan, Jerry on the Job, Krazy Kat, Bring Up Father, Jimmy*, and Tom Power's fanciful *Joys and Glooms* at their command."

The article noted that Edgar B. Hatrick, who had direct charge over the animated cartoon department at International, stated the term "cartoon" would be replaced by "animated comedies." Gregory La Cava chimed in with the amount of labor involved in creating animation.

"We are taking as much pains with these animated comedies as is ordinarily taken with a five-reel feature," La Cava said. "The scenarios are written and rewritten with the utmost care, and each character is faithfully worked out by some different artist so that each one of the little actors has an individuality of his own."

La Cava stated that many critics who previewed the *Happy Hooligan* cartoon, *The Tale of a Monkey,* declared it "ranks as strong in delicious comedy as the famous story of *Androcles and The Lion.*"

"It is the desire of International to impress upon the exhibitor as well as upon the public that these comedies have long since passed the experimental stage and we are worthy of a place on any program," La Cava added.

Toward the end of the year, International hired John C. Terry to join the staff as a full-time animator. Previously, Terry had managed Cartoon Film Service, Inc.

Happy Hooligan's first full year in animation had been well received, and was adored by the general public. Aside from the stable platform presence of the ongoing Frederick Opper *Happy Hooligan* comic strip, the cartoons had actually had a reverse effect, increasing the character's popularity in comics.

This translated into the news in a variety of ways. While many grassroots level expressions of admiration were unauthorized, Hearst and Opper didn't care, as long as they were sincere, without financial intentions, bordering on copyright infringement.

In mid-January, citizens of North Platte, Nebraska staged a *Katzenjammer Kids* community picnic. Among the many "guests," persons dressed in costumes of popular characters, was Happy Hooligan.

In late September, The Boy Scouts in Chautauqua, Kansas, held a circus event that featured look-alikes of Cinderella, Charles Chaplin, Uncle Sam and Happy Hooligan. The area newspaper, *The Liberal Democrat*, reported the celebration was "a screaming success."

> Billy Joy is everything her name implies and has a clever run of song and chatter. The Spanish Goldins, billed as "Europe's most sensational entertainers," are hardly that. Stone and King can sing and dance a little, and the novelty musical act of Fargo and Wells gets across. The Lonesome Luke comedy and the Happy Hooligan cartoon tend to liven up the program.

Godwin Weekly's June 23, 1917 article.

The Richmond Palladium newspaper sponsored a contest where youths were encouraged to submit a fictional story, with the winner seeing his or her work published. One Indiana boy, William Bennett, a seventh grader, won with his seaworthy tale featuring Frederick Opper's Gaston, Alphonso and Happy Hooligan as principal characters. Bennett's story appeared in the December 17 edition of the newspaper.

One example of the popularity of *Happy Hooligan* cartoons surfaced in the pages of *Godwin's Weekly*, on June 23. A Salt Lake City, Utah, theater, The Liberty, owed something to Frederick Opper, observing a less than enthusiastic response to a live play performances on stage.

"The *Happy Hooligan* cartoon tends to liven up the program," *Godwin's Weekly* reported.

Happy Hooligan's popularity infiltrated the world of social and political dialogue, as well.

On February 4, the *New York Tribune* published an opinion piece by Robert C. Benchley, targeting humor that was once acceptable, but now frowned upon.

"The tramp joke has gone, too," Benchley wrote. "It wasn't so very long ago that a tramp with a tomato can tied around his waist was sure-fire. Just why the tomato can, though, I have never been able to understand. But its survival today is seen in *Happy Hooligan*, the one exception that proves the rule."

The Mississippi newspaper, the *Grenada Sentinel*, lashed out at a former state governor in an August 31 editorial, stating if he stayed in a Senate race, "he will play the part of Happy Hooligan. Political crocodiles will get him before he even starts upstream."

The year 1918 would be a big one for the increase of quality and popularity of *Happy Hooligan* cartoons. But with it came the death spiral of International Film Service.

CHAPTER SIX
1918 Happy Hooligan Cartoons

At the dawn of the new year, Pathé Exchange, Inc., issued a statement addressing the importance of story content, and quality in cartoons. *Motion Picture News* presented the announcement on January 26.

"When Pathé presented the first successful animated cartoons some years ago, almost any animated cartoon could get by on the strength of the novelty alone," a Pathé official stated. "Audiences wondered how the effects were obtained, and we received scores of queries asking for a detailed statement as to how the thing was accomplished. Animated cartoons now, however, are no longer a novelty. They need real comedy scenarios behind them. They need production, smoothness, finish. They need a humorist to conceive them and experts to animate them. The crudeness of conception and execution is not tolerated."

Pathé pointed to the first *Happy Hooligan* animated short of the new year as an example of meeting the new quality standards.

"At this office, we go on record as saying in our opinion, the *Happy Hooligan* cartoon, *Hearts and Horses*, released on January 13, is the funniest animated cartoon that has ever been made," the official said.

The new *Happy Hooligan* cartoon, *Hearts and Horses*, injects the ho-

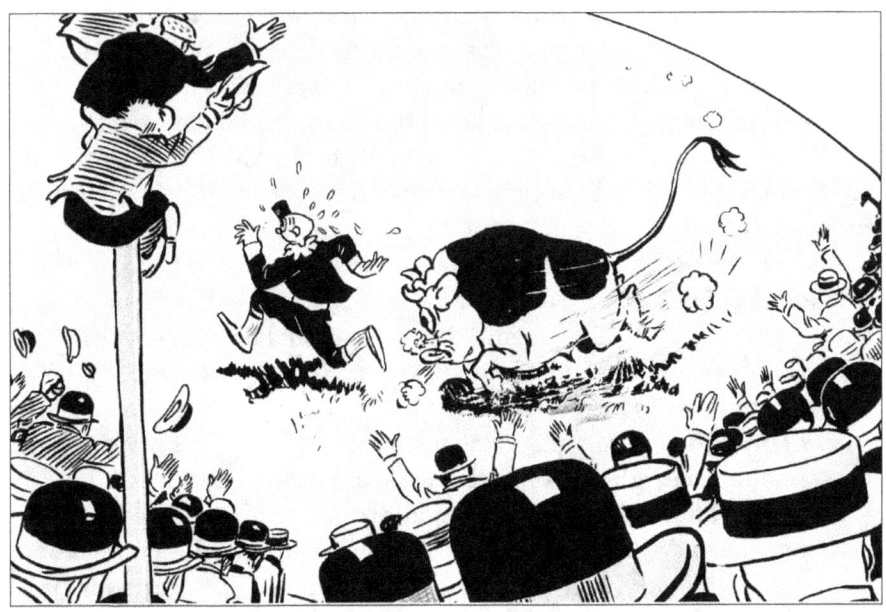

Illustration from the *Happy Hooligan* cartoon *Throwing the Bull*, released June 17, 1918

bo into the wild world of horse racing. In the story, which takes place at the racetrack, Happy rides an old-time favorite to victory. The quality of animation in the film exceeded previous *Happy Hooligan* cartoons. The improvement didn't go unnoticed by critics.

"This features *Happy Hooligan* and the boys in a rather elaborate animated drawing," *Moving Picture World* reported on January 19. "The handling of great crowds in constant movement is quite an achievement as here presented. It is very funny."

Many cartoons of the era contained racist images, and *Happy Hooligan* comedy shorts weren't exempt from the practice. Some of the tramp's earlier animated shorts depicted African-Americans peripherally, acting silly. However, the next *Happy Hooligan* cartoon, the 19th in the series, was blatantly racist on many levels.

The *Happy Hooligan* cartoon, *All For the Ladies*, released on February 10, opens with a scene depicting two kids dipping a "small black person" in a bucket of water to "make ink." But, the cruel act doesn't go unchecked. Hooligan rebukes the youngsters for their conduct and sits them down to tell them a story.

The tale he conveys as a "lesson" portrays Native-Americans as black arts practitioners. The fable features a young woman who is a snake charmer that keeps a batch of the slinky serpents as pets.

"*All for the Ladies* tells a wonderful tale of a border raid, a lady with a swastika, and a band of slithery snakes," *Motion Picture News* reported on February 16. The swastika was used by ancient *Native Americans* of the Mississippian culture, and was not yet a Nazi symbol.

Moving Picture World also praised the cartoon on February 16.

"*Happy Hooligan* tells a wonderful story to the kids," the *News* said. "His adventures with the Indian squaw and her pet snakes is extremely funny. An excellent subject."

All For the Ladies was the final film circulated by Pathé that year. William Randolph Hearst dumped the distributor for their cartoon line and entered into an agreement with Education Films Corporation of America to distribute the animated shorts. Hearst did retain Pathé as the distributor of its newsreel films.

The Dramatic Mirror magazine was just one of several publications that announced the details of the business association on April 6.

"The Educational Films Corporation of America announces through president Earle W. Hammons that it has just acquired sole releasing rights to the *Happy Hooligan* and *Katzenjammer Kids* cartoons produced by the International Film Company, widely known through the

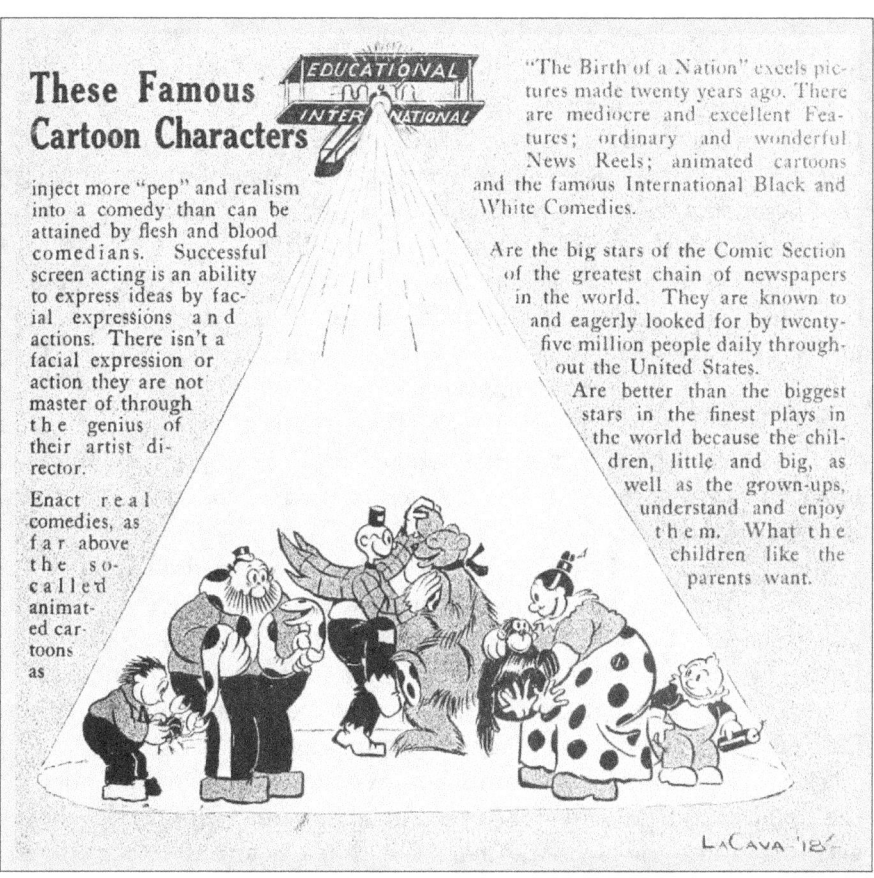

These Famous Cartoon Characters inject more "pep" and realism into a comedy than can be attained by flesh and blood comedians. Successful screen acting is an ability to express ideas by facial expressions and actions. There isn't a facial expression or action they are not master of through the genius of their artist director.

Enact real comedies, as far above the so-called animated cartoons as

"The Birth of a Nation" excels pictures made twenty years ago. There are mediocre and excellent Features; ordinary and wonderful News Reels; animated cartoons and the famous International Black and White Comedies.

Are the big stars of the Comic Section of the greatest chain of newspapers in the world. They are known to and eagerly looked for by twenty-five million people daily throughout the United States.

Are better than the biggest stars in the finest plays in the world because the children, little and big, as well as the grown-ups, understand and enjoy them. What the children like the parents want.

LaCava '18

A 1918 advertisement promoting International Film Service partnering with Educational Films Corporation of America.

medium of the Hearst newspapers," the Mirror reported. "The first release of the cartoons under the new management will be on April 15."

Earle W. Hammons spoke in the piece about how the cartoons were part of a bigger package that featured travelogues and educational films. The cartoons routinely appeared at the end of the feature reels.

"We have noticed for some time that these cartoons were increasing in interest and real artistic merit," Hammons said. "We were gratified when the International Film Company asked us to become the controlling factor in their distribution. We confidently expect that they will take their place with the *Bruce Scenics* and *Ditmars Living Book of Nature* films, issued by us, as genuine short features."

Doing His Bit, next *Happy Hooligan* animated cartoon, deposits the tramp into the war effort. Released on April 29, it was the first in the series distributed by Education Films Corporation of America.

In the story, Happy Hooligan is captured by the enemy army and forced to stand guard at a German post. He makes his escape by painting his shadow in black on a wall. The German commander, engaged in flirting with a young lady, is satisfied, after giving a glance back, that Happy is still there. The tramp becomes a one-man war machine disrupting enemy submariners, German aircraft, and concludes with him dropping a bomb on the Kaiser, making him a hero.

"Happy tames torpedoes and turns them against their makers, upsets the calculations and afternoon coffee of the enemy aerial navigators, and has the war just about coming to a polite and pleasing ending," *Motion Picture News* reported on May 4.

Moving Picture World also praised the cartoon in its May 11 edition.

"*Doing His Bit*, the *Happy Hooligan* cartoon is exceptionally funny," the magazine reported. "He does his bit in a manner that has never been thought of by other heroes."

Happy Hooligan in *Throwing the Bull*, was released on June 17. In the story, Happy plays the custodian of a cow that yields condensed milk. Happy is occupied, being romanced by a female Spanish dancer, the cow is stolen and deposited in an arena for matadors to battle. The number of fighting bulls has dwindled, and the bovine will do. With a little prodding and training, the cow becomes aggressive.

The Mexican bullring features hundreds of animated spectators in the stands. Hooligan enters the ring and tries to tame the cow. The hobo gets tossed into the air more than a few times, before the savage beast settles, and Happy returns him to his barn.

Theaters, routinely supplied with sheet music for *Happy Hooligan* cartoons, performed some amusing numbers on the house keyboard for *Throwing the Bull*. Included was a hoochie-coochie tune for a Spanish dance routine, and a rhythmic Toreador number for the arena scene.

"There was plenty of action on the part of both Happy and the bull, and a wonderful Mexican lady dancer, whose movements would rival the slithery snake in sinuosity," *Motion Picture News* reported on July 6. "Really, the cleverness of those chaps who made the little drawings that compose a cartoon and of the man who arranges the footage and exposures, and all the details that go for smooth animation is beyond admiration and almost beyond belief."

Motion Picture World also praised the cartoon in its June 29 edition.

"Many things happen to the cow, and to Happy, in his endeavors to return it to the more peaceful pursuit," the magazine stated.

Happy was in the money in his next cartoon, *Mopping Up a Million*,

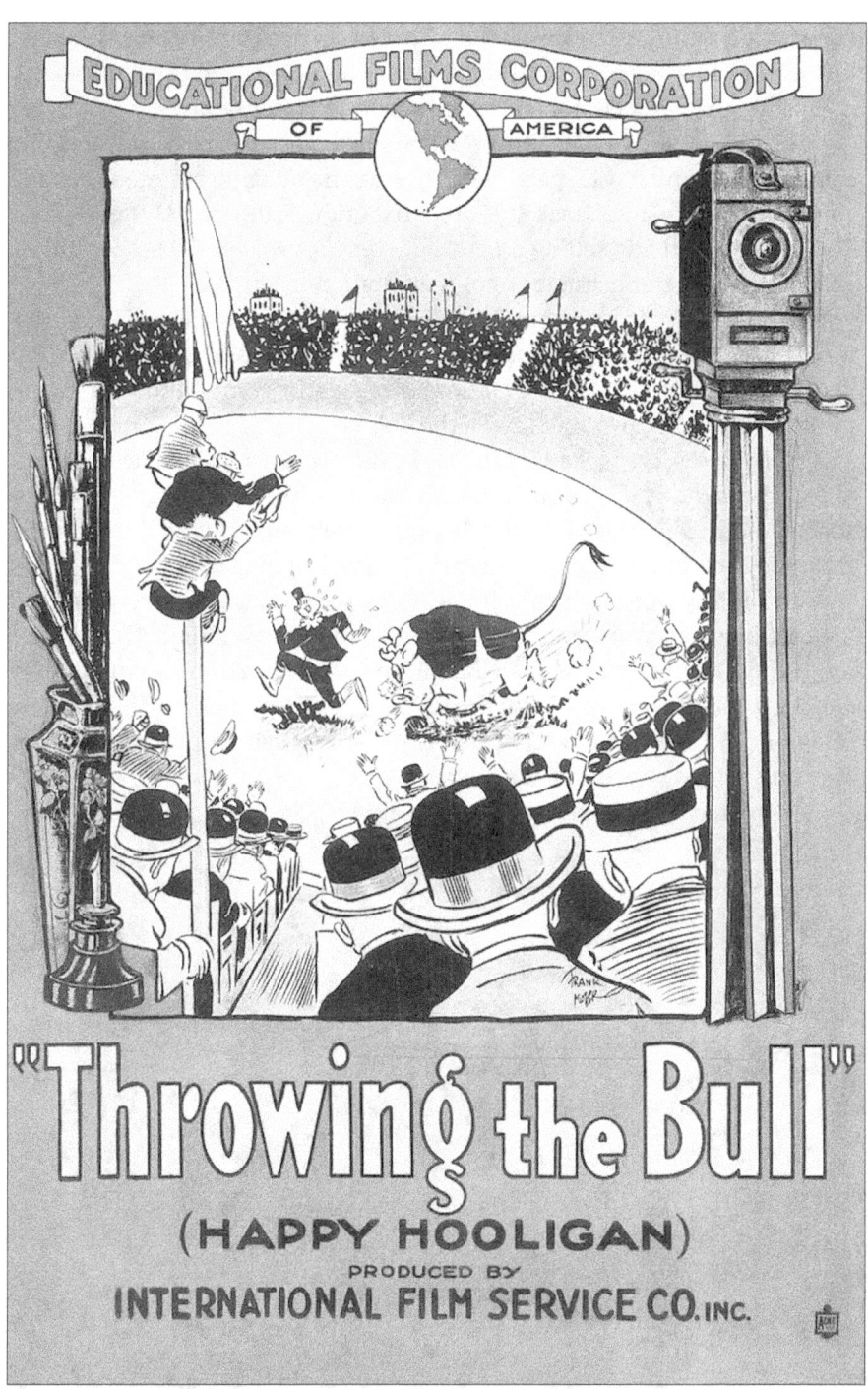

Poster promoting the *Happy Hooligan* cartoon *Throwing the Bull*, released June 17, 1918

released on July 22. However, the fortune was prize money for stepping into a ring for a spirited wrestling match. The only spectators enthusiastic for the mismatched hobo were very agitated pack of dogs.

Educational Films Corporation launched an expensive advertising campaign, running full-page advertisements in entertainment magazines, highlighting their exclusive distribution rights for IFS cartoons. They also placed ads selling a new, lightweight projector, The Zenith, to encourage the establishment of new exhibition locations.

Released August 5, *Happy Hooligan* in *His Dark Past*, places the tramp back in a time he would rather forget. Appearing on August 12, *Tramp! Tramp! Tramp!* offers some pretty stiff competition for Happy, in a quest to crown the king of the hobos.

A Bold Bad Man picked up praise in the press and a key promotional feature spot. The *Happy Hooligan* cartoon, released August 19, was subsequently showcased in a full-page article containing illustrations from the film, in the December issue of *Film Fun* magazine.

Motion Picture News praised the cartoon in two October reviews.

"Certainly everyone goes away from the theatre laughing after watching Happy Hooligan in *A Bold Bad Man*," the magazine reported. "His efforts to outdo [actors] William S. Hart, and Douglas Fairbanks, are said to be as funny as anything Gregory La Cava has ever hit upon in his amusing satires of present-day fads."

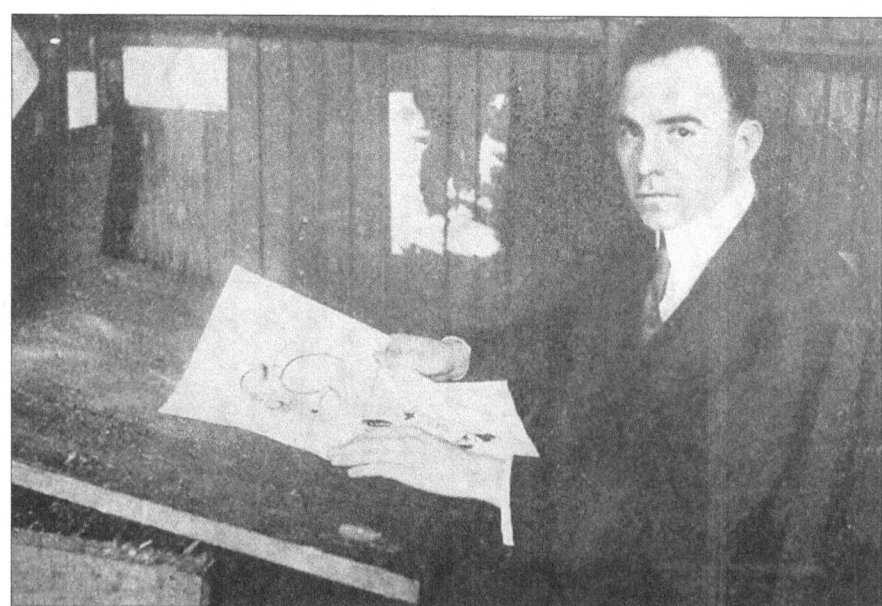

Gregory La Cava, working at International Film Service, May 1918.

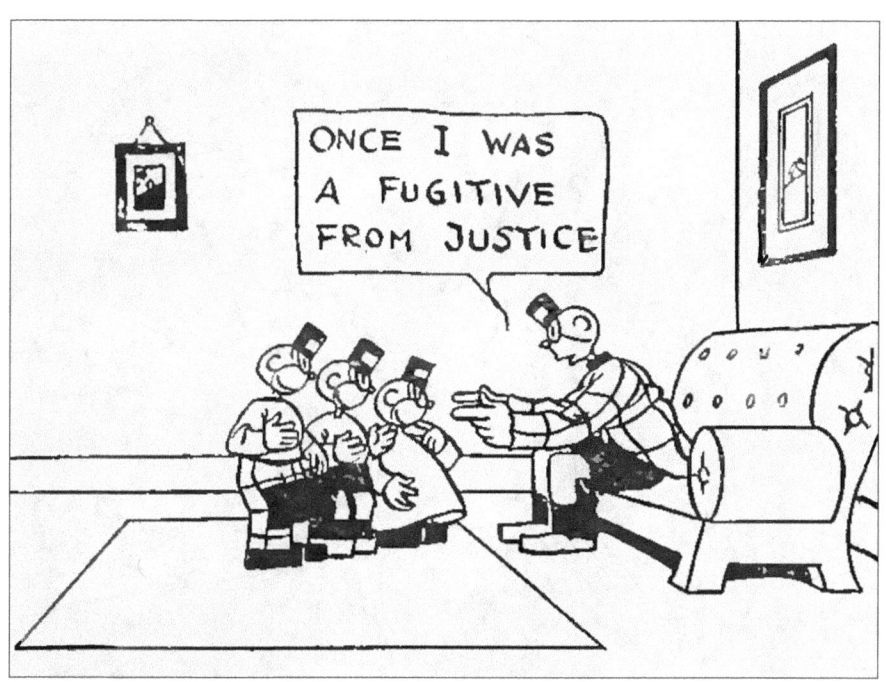

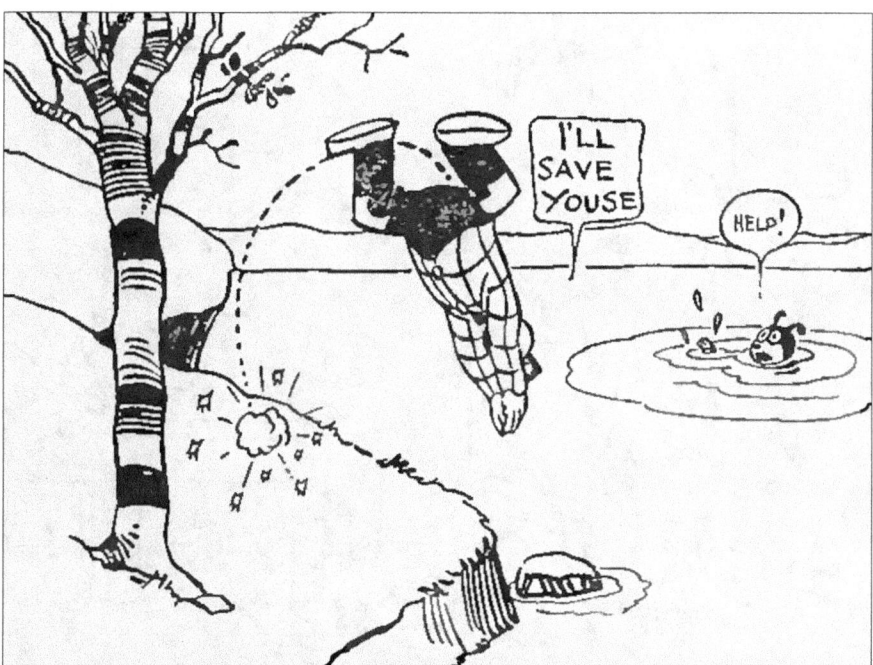

Illustrations from the *Happy Hooligan* cartoon, *A Bold Bad Man*, released August 19, 1918. Series of artwork in chronological order. Top, Happy begins telling is tall Western tale to his nephews. Above, Happy dives into a lake to rescue a drowning hound.

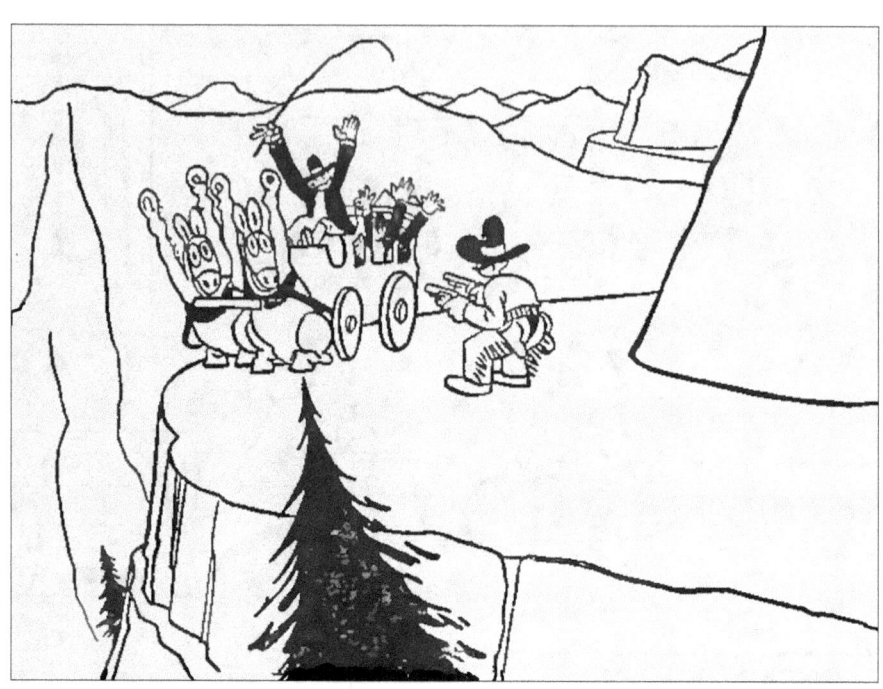

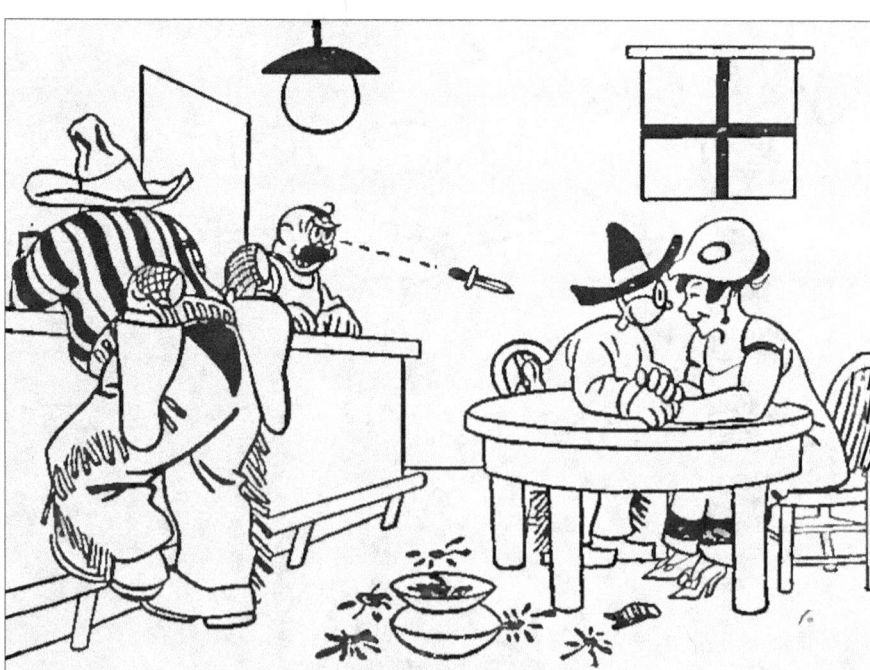

Illustrations from the *Happy Hooligan* cartoon, *A Bold Bad Man*, released August 19, 1918. Series of artwork in chronological order. Top, highwayman Happy holding up a stagecoach. Above, an angry barkeeper spies Happy flirting with his girlfriend.

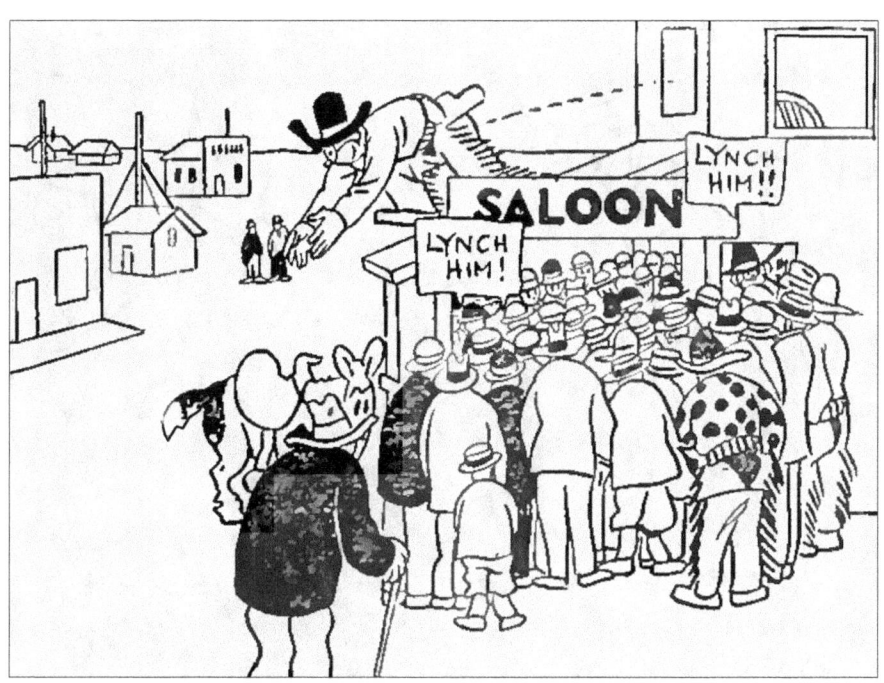

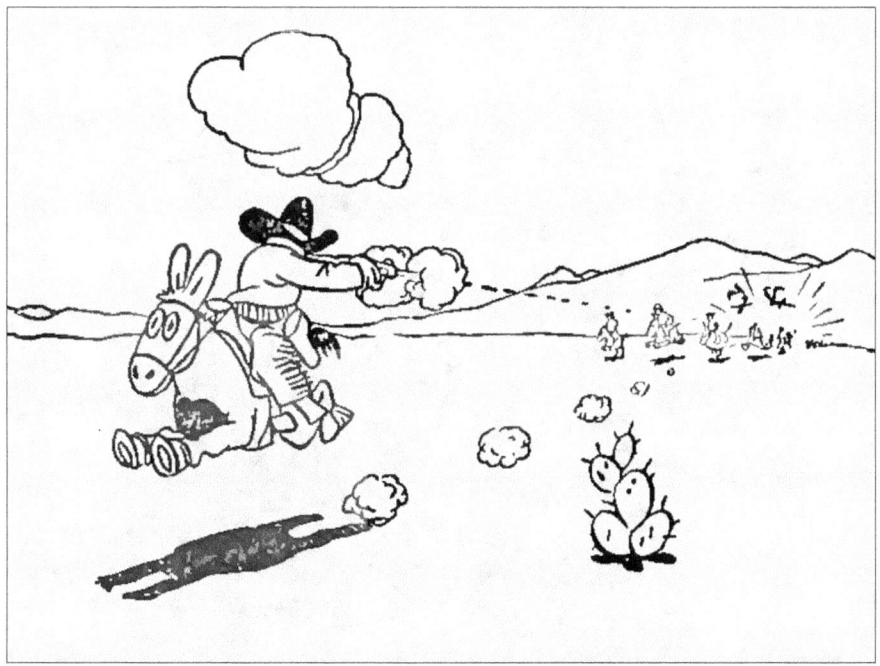

Illustrations from the *Happy Hooligan* cartoon, *A Bold Bad Man*, released August 19, 1918. Series of artwork in chronological order. Top, Happy exits the saloon as an angry lynch mob forms below. Above, being pursued, Happy fires back at the Sheriff and his posse crossing the desert.

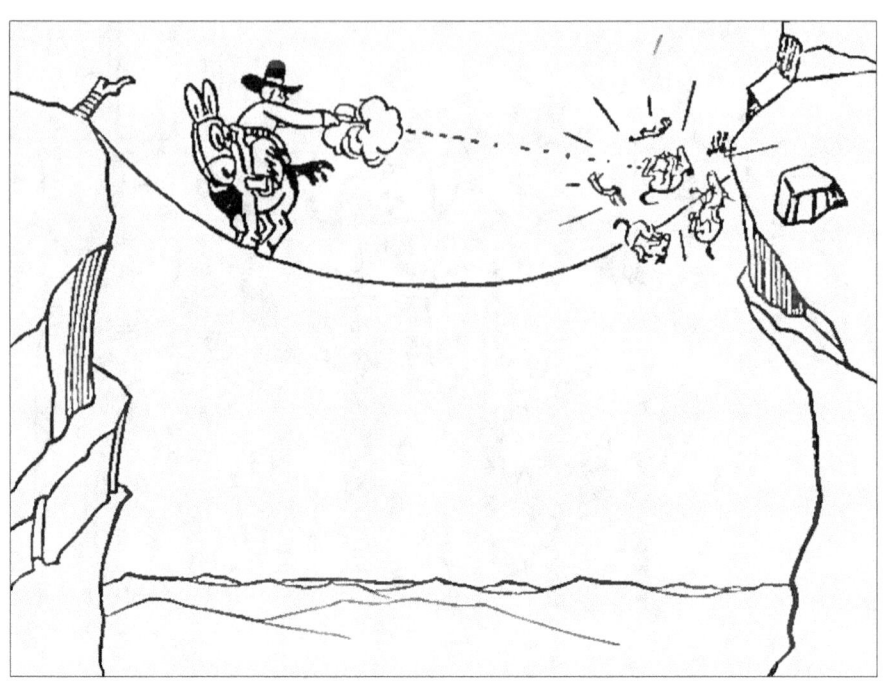

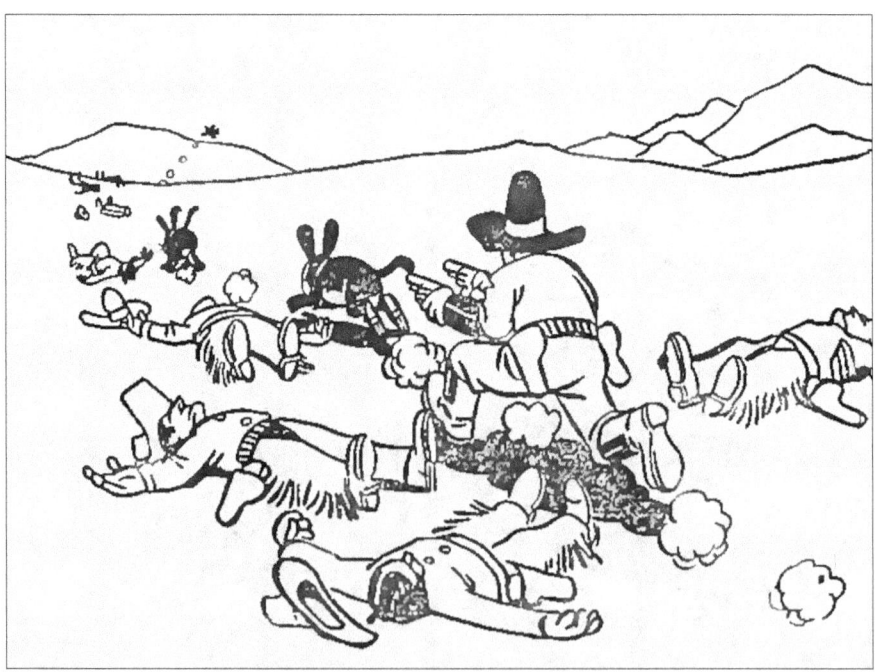

Illustrations from the *Happy Hooligan* cartoon, *A Bold Bad Man*, released August 19, 1918. Series of artwork in chronological order. Top, Happy's high wire act, crossing a gorge on horseback. Above, Happy leaves the Sheriff and posse behind in the dust, but the hound continues the chase.

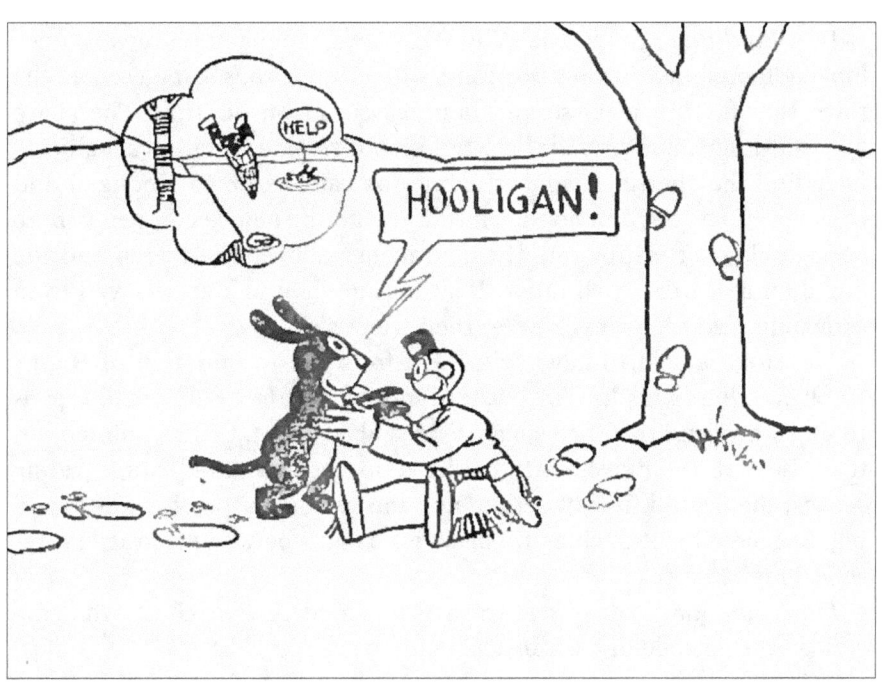

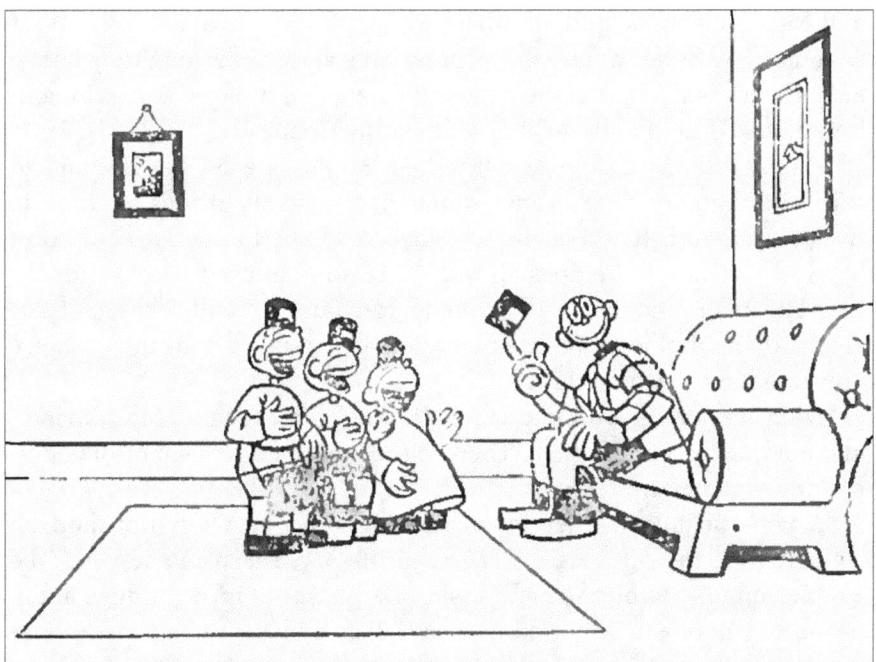

Illustrations from the *Happy Hooligan* cartoon, *A Bold Bad Man*, released August 19, 1918. Series of artwork in chronological order. Top, the remaining member of the posse catches Happy, and turns out to be the hound he rescued. Above, Happy's nephews laugh, and don't believe him.

In *A Bold Bad Man*, set in Wild West days, Hooligan rescues an odd-looking bloodhound from drowning. After Happy robs a stagecoach, the town sheriff, with a posse and hounds, is hot on his trail. The chase spans a desert, and one by one, the mob dissipates due to casualties—including the sheriff. A sole tracking dog catches up to Hooligan and runs him up a tree. But some snuff in the hound's nose compels him to sneeze, blowing Happy out of the branches above. The tramp and the dog then recognize each other. It's the same hound Happy saved from drowning, and the pair rekindles their friendship.

The story is said to have originated from the imagination of Happy Hooligan, due to his love of Western motion pictures. The popular genre was a proven box office success since about 1914. Critics pointed out that the natural movements depicted in the animated horse riding scenes, the overall flow of action, and the use of perspective was amazing. Special effects, such as firearms exchanges between characters, received high marks.

Film Fun magazine's feature article, titled *A Bold Bad Man*, described the episode in a whimsical manner.

"Westward the course of comedy wings its way. Indeed, the Bill Harts and Nate Salisburys, and all others who wish us to take our Wild West seriously had better organize a counter attack, or, first thing they know, an audience will laugh in their most thrilling reel because some thing in it reminds them of Fatty Arbuckle or Happy Hooligan.

"Happy is the latest movie star to take Horace Greeley's advice and go West. Accompanying are views which give some slight idea of what he does to and with the West in *A Bold Bad Man*. No one is required to 'double' for Happy; he does all the hard stunts himself without flinching. The man who made the tomato can famous, with characteristic Hooligan helpfulness, rescues a strange bloodhound from a watery grave; that by way of prelude.

"Later he doffs his tomato can for a sombrero, turning highwayman and holding up a mail coach. There is the hands-up realism of the horses in moving picture.

"A pen-and-ink frontier town becomes too warm for him, and he 'animates' to the open desert. The sheriff—a Western movie would be Hamlet-minus-Hamlet without a sheriff—pursues him with dogs and a posse, but Hooligan scatters Snuff as well as bullets in his getaway, and the posse suffers severe casualties.

"Hooligan is finally treed, but a violent, Snuff-inspired sneeze by a relentless bloodhound, last of the pursuers, shakes Happy loose from his hold and he falls. Then occurs a Bernard Shaw *Androcles and the Lion* finish; the relentless bloodhound recognizes in Hooligan the man who saved him from drowning. There is a specially inset [thought balloon] called to the graphic for a 'flashback' in picture, whereupon all ends happily and Hooliganly."

The next *Happy Hooligan* cartoon, *The Latest in Underwear*, , hit theaters on August 26. In the story, Happy Hooligan cleans up alongside a Chinese laundryman, an African-American washer-woman, and a billy goat. But what he is "cleaning up on" is garments he is stealing off a clothesline. This compels a detective to investigate the case to uncover the culprit.

"This is truly a black-and-white rumpus comedy," *Motion Picture News* reported.

Not only was the laundry hung out to dry, *Happy Hooligan* was on the line, figuratively speaking. The fast pace of new films came to an abrupt halt with the release of *The Latest in Underwear*. The next new *Happy Hooligan* cartoon wouldn't be issued until October.

Little did the public know that chaos resided inside the offices of International Film Service. William Randolph Hearst's longtime pro-Germany position had come back to haunt him after the United States entered World War I on April 6, 1917.

While Hearst had long since created distance between his news operation and civility toward Germany prior to America's engagement it had been too little, too late. Newspaper sales dropped and subscribers had cancelled.

Hearst's entire operation had entered a death spiral of enormous debt for other monumental reasons. According to IFS general manager, Carl E. Zittel, the studio was, "thoroughly demoralized by the influenza [pandemic] and the demands for military service." No one will go to the movies when the Federal government has told people to stay home.

Larger film studios survived the hit, but IFS, running on a thin profit margin, could not. Compounding the crisis, Educational Films Corporation of America had ceased distributing Hearst cartoons.

"Up to the time of the outbreak of the Spanish influenza, we had been distributing International's animated cartoons with great success," EFC president, Earle W. Hammons, later said. "But when the situation reached a critical stage, Educational ceased releasing these cartoons, and subsequently the International Film Service stopped making them."

Which is exactly what happened next. To cut his losses, Hearst moved to eliminate his least profitable business, IFS. The entire staff was laid off on July 6. Historically, the date is known as "Black Monday" in the animation world.

Still believing in his animation line, Hearst approached animator John C. Terry with a licensing agreement. Hearst commissioned Terry to assemble a new studio to continue production of the cartoons left on the drawing boards. Some former IFS staffers were rehired, finding work at Terry's Greenwich Village studio. The move was an act of dumping liabilities, validating write-offs, and a restructuring IFS. Maintaining ownership and oversight, Hearst began to rebuild, and, restore his animation division back to what it had been.

The halt in production resulted in the next pair of Happy Hooligan cartoons not appearing until mid-fall. With the absence of Educational Films Corporation of America, IFS had no distributor. Efforts by manager Carl E. Zittel to establish a Hearst film exchange failed to materialize. William Randolph Hearst contacted Pathé Exchange, which already distributed his newsreels, to once again circulate his cartoons.

The arrangement allowed IFS cartoons to begin its comeback.

Happy Hooligan in *Smash-Up in China*, released on October 21, presented Happy as an ambassador, placing him in China during an uprising. With the abduction of the Prime Minister, Happy pursues the kidnappers, rescues the Prime Minister, and using a potion, cures him of an affliction.

For saving the Prime Minister, the Chinese President rewards Happy by knighting him. He also places a special garter around the hobo's ankle and dubs him "the Poiple [purple] Sock-Holder."

Displaying a leap in animation pictorially, *Smash-Up in China* displayed some amazing perspective views, such an army of soldiers marching up the Great Wall, and Happy flying, back and forth, with a propeller on his rear, in aerial combat with the Prime Minister's kidnappers. Adding amusement, the enemy dirigible bore the marking of a pirate ship, including a Jolly Roger skull and crossbones logo and flag.

The cartoon also featured a travelogue-like quality, showing Chinese architecture, landscapes, and cultural traditions.

"It's an amazing story of how Happy Hooligan cures the monarch of gout and wins the order of the 'Knight of Garter,'" *Motion Picture News* reported on October 26.

Ten original illustrations from *Happy Hooligan* in *Smash-Up in China* appeared in the November issue of *Film Fun* magazine. Each image was accompanied by a caption placed beneath it, telling the story, much like a newspaper comic page.

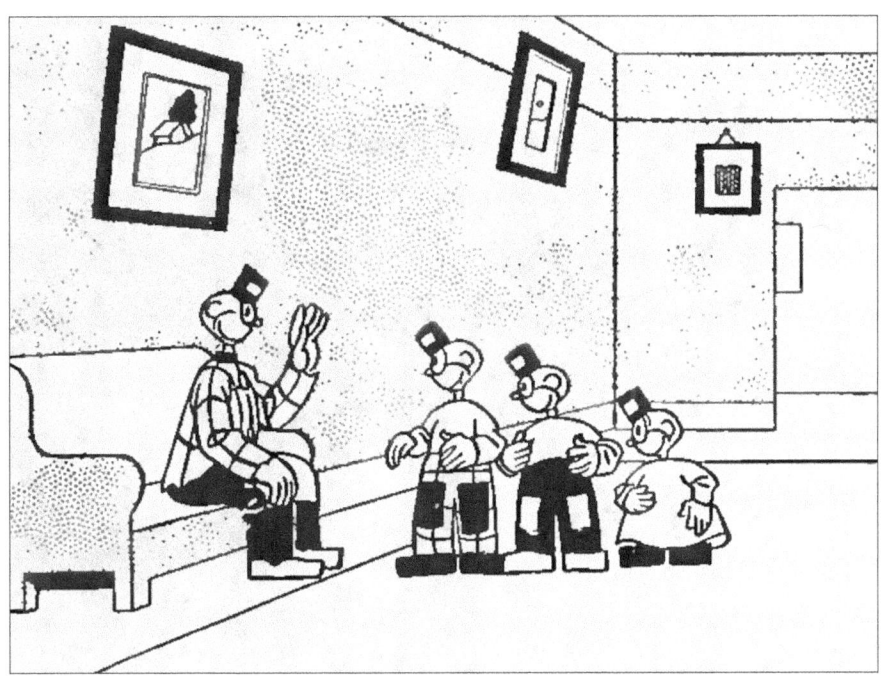

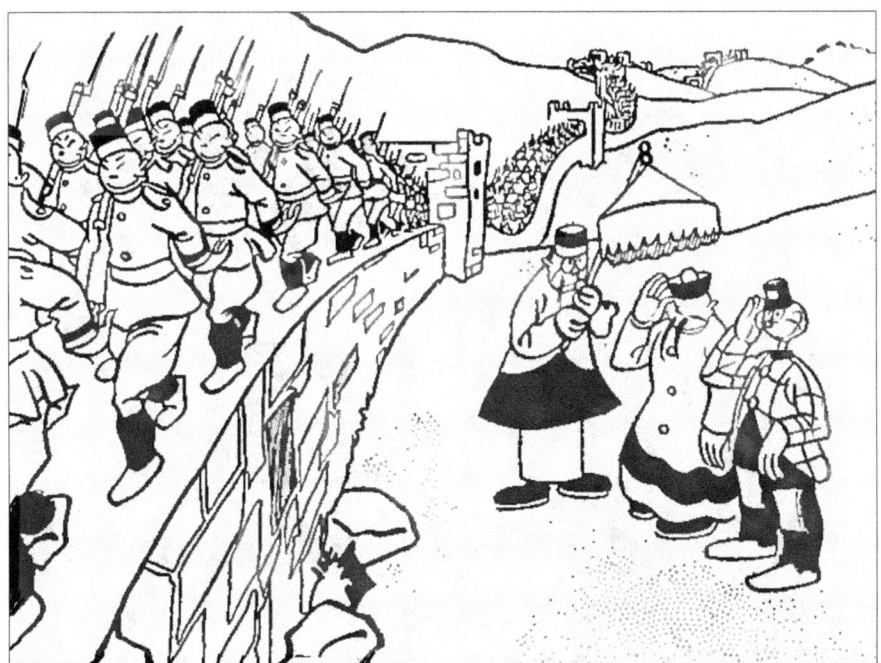

Illustrations from the *Happy Hooligan* cartoon, *Smash-Up in China*, released October 21, 1918. Series of artwork in chronological order. Top, Happy begins to tell his nephews the story about his trip to China. Above, Happy, with the Prime Minister, revues troops on The Great Wall.

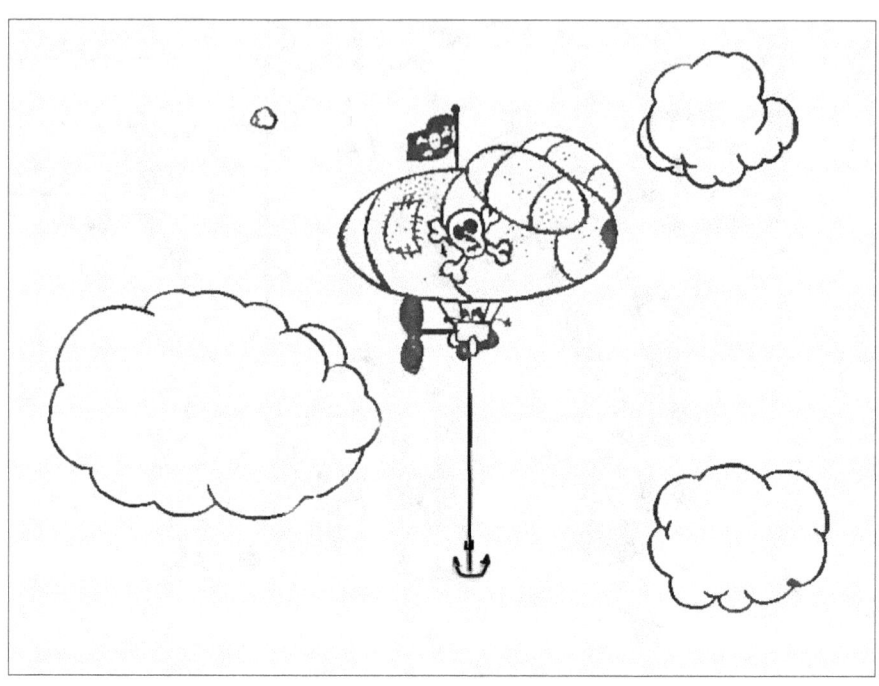

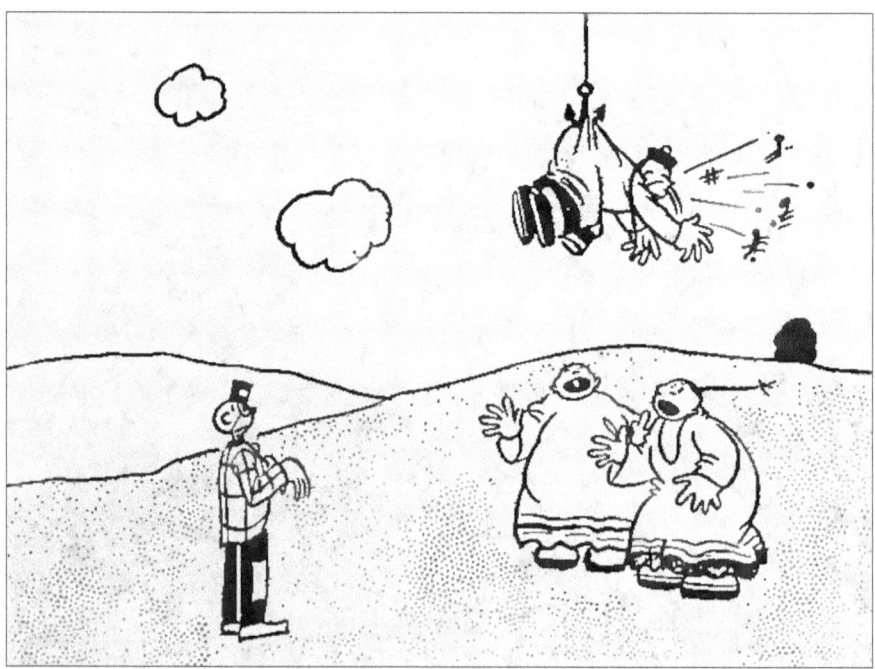

Illustrations from the *Happy Hooligan* cartoon, *Smash-Up in China*, released October 21, 1918. Series of artwork in chronological order. Top, A flying Chinese "air-junk" out fishing. Above, the airship hooks its target, abducting the Prime Minister. An uprising is afoot.

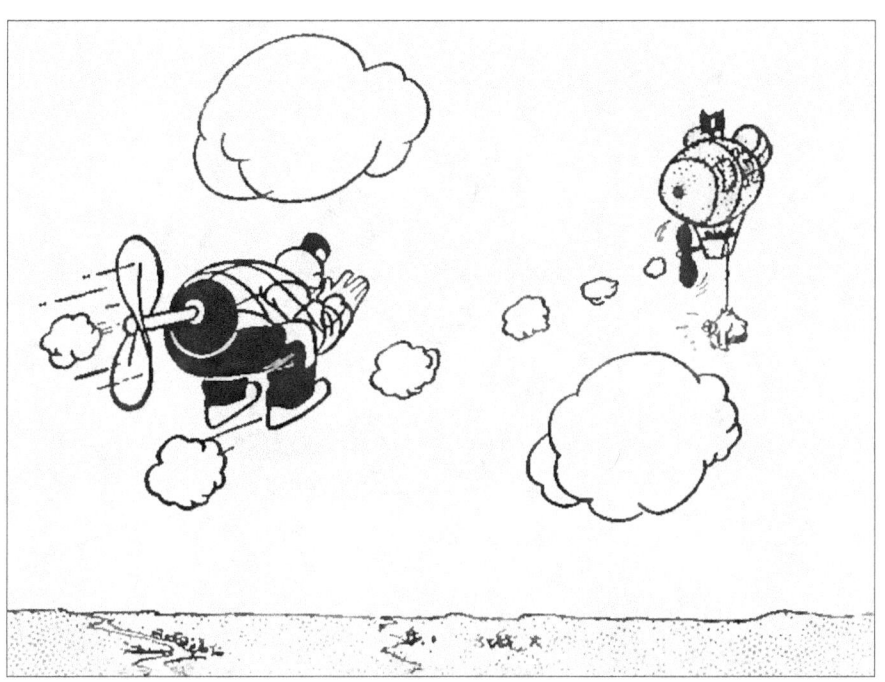

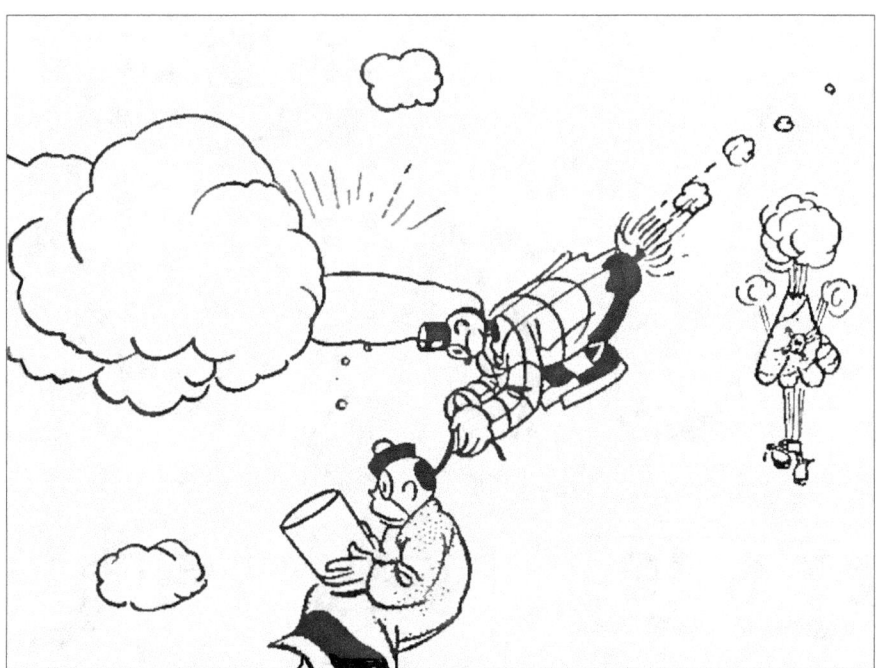

Illustrations from the *Happy Hooligan* cartoon, *Smash-Up in China*, released October 21, 1918. Series of artwork in chronological order. Top, with a propeller on his rear, Happy takes of after the kidnappers. Above, Happy rescues the leader, and administers first aid.

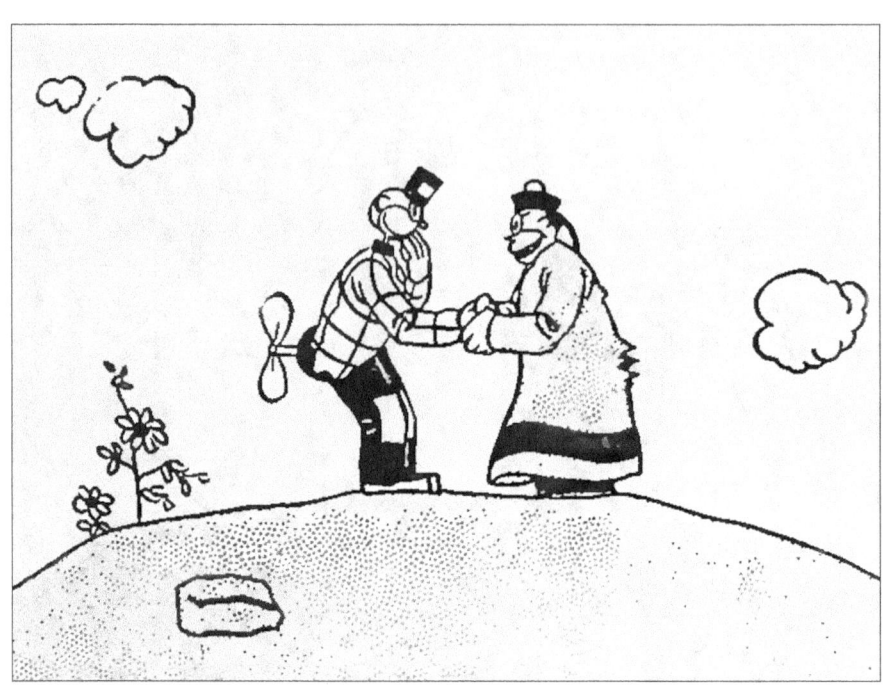

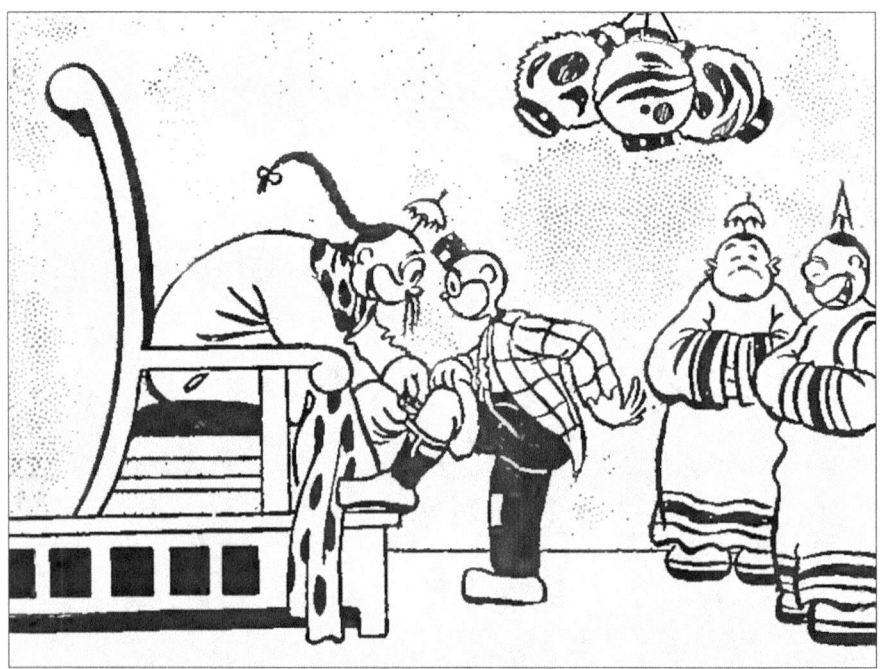

Illustrations from the *Happy Hooligan* cartoon, *Smash-Up in China*, released October 21, 1918. Series of artwork in chronological order. Top, the grateful Prime Minster thanks Happy. Above, the President of China knights Happy, and places a special garter on his leg as an award.

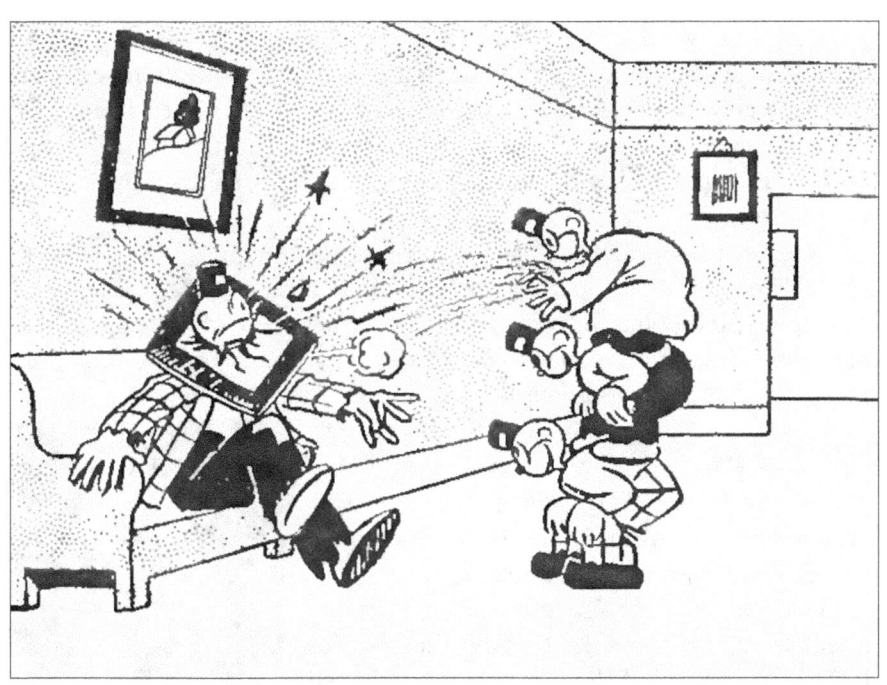

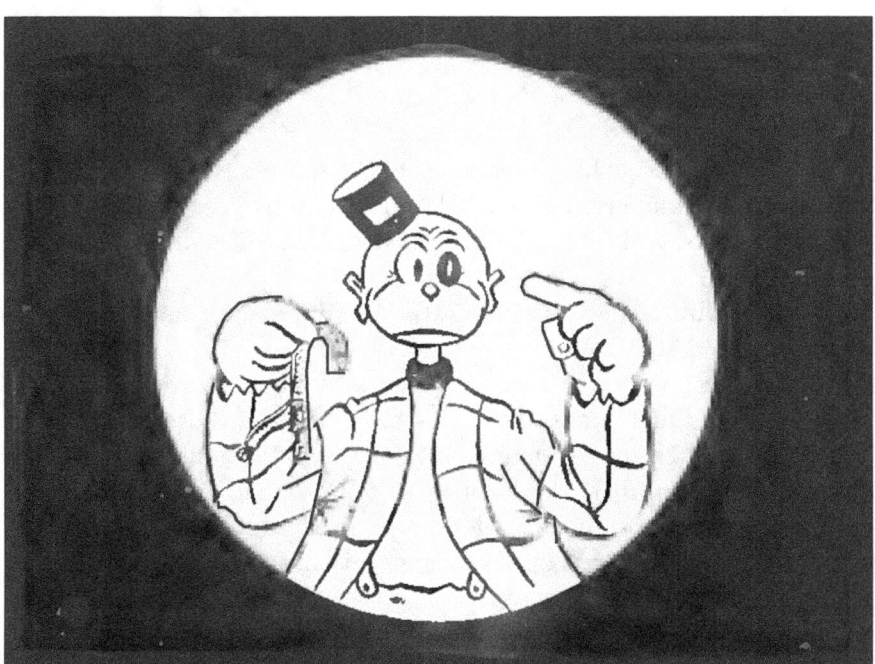

Illustrations from the *Happy Hooligan* cartoon, *Smash-Up in China*, released October 21, 1918. Series of artwork in chronological order. Top, his nephews don't believe him, and "frame" their uncle. Above, Happy shows off his black eye, and knighthood "decoration," closing the tale.

At the time William Randolph Hearst was working to restructure his cartoon business, an animated film created by one of his employees was receiving glowing reviews. *The Sinking of the Lusitania*, spearheaded by Winsor McCay, had steadily gained momentum since its release on July 20. The 12-minute film invoked a national wave a patriotism during the wartime effort.

Hearst's pro-Germany stance was the reason comics artist Winsor McCay declined to be part of International Film Service's animation catalogue. McCay had been listed in the earliest IFS advertisements as one of the Hearst cartoonists whose creations would join the lineup in 1916. But, no McCay cartoons ever appeared.

When the RMS Lusitania was torpedoed by a German U-boat on May 7, 1915, Hearst downplayed the event. The slight outraged McCay because he had been forced by Hearst to do anti-British and anti-war cartoons.

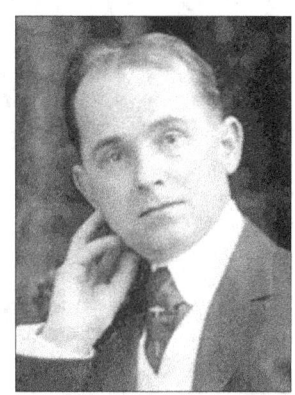

The Sinking of the Lusitania wasn't created with assistance from IFS. Nor did they release it. McCay drew all of the illustrations and used the Vitagraph Studios facilities for photography. He financed the entire project himself. Jewel Productions distributed the film to theaters.

Winsor McCay.

Perhaps to manage his late support of the war effort, Hearst newspapers published and syndicated a column written by Frederick Opper, in support of Liberty Loans. The article was titled *The Power That Puts Men Down*.

In the column, appearing in mid-October, Frederick Opper reflected on history, and how justice will prevail.

"Too much power has been the ruination of almost every man who has had it. It brought Caesar to the assassins' knives. It brought Wolsey, who had been the greatest man in all Europe, to the abbey of Leicester, impoverished and disgraced, to beg a cot to die on. It brought Bonaparte, who had more power than any man who ever lived, before or since, to end his career, cooped on a lonely island, digging in a little garden to keep his fat down.

"That is what too much power can do for big brains. What it can do for little brains we see in the German Kaiser, watching today the wrecking of all his foolish, brutal plans of world conquest.

"It does not need a great stretch of imagination to picture an international military court-martial sitting in Berlin, not a great while from now. It is presided over by Marshal Foch and with him are the greatest generals of America, England, France, Italy and Belgium. At the prisoners bar stands William Honen Zollern, the dethroned Emperor of Germany, and his son, the ex-Crown Prince. These two, the greatest criminals in all history, are awaiting sentence.

"That sentence will be just, pitiless and terrible. And after them will come to the bar, one after the other, all the Kaiser's ruthless, slaughtering commanders, and his wretched, culpable dupe, the ex-Emperor of Austria, to meet retribution for their countless murders and barbarities.

"And all this is being made possible by the help of America's superb soldiers and sailors and the great nation behind them, ready with its money and its encouragement. And that money and that encouragement must never fail them. The Hun must be beaten.

"Every Liberty Loan must be sustained so that we may all look ahead with confidence to that proud day, that day of victory, 'when the boys come home.'"

Suspension of the *Happy Hooligan* animation schedule occurred after the release of *Smash-Up in China*. A new animated cartoon of the hobo would not surface until February, the following year. With it would arise a reconstituted International Film Service cartoon studio.

Even under tremendous circumstances, International Film Service's animation department had achieved incredible popularity in 1918. Not only had the animation process vastly improved, but the attention to clever and humorous stories had offered mainstream comedies that just happened to be animated.

While the Pathé Exchange, Inc. had agreed to distribute the few cartoon titles IFS issued that fall, the experience hadn't been cordial between the two. Thus, Hearst threw Pathé under the bus.

The Hearst organization announced that after December 24, Pathé Exchange, Inc. would no longer be distributing its newsreels. News films after that point would carry only the Hearst International News name. That would subsequently change the end of 1919, when a consolidation created Hearst's International Film Service, Inc.

Hearst, which had maintained an association acquiring film news content from Universal Current Events and Mutual Screen Telegram, retained those resources.

The year 1919 would restore IFS, but then see it dissolved, leasing its cartoon properties to Bray Productions under an agreement with Goldwyn.

CHAPTER SEVEN
1919 Happy Hooligan Cartoons

The reboot of the International Film Service animation department, also branded International Comedies in Black and White, produced a more streamlined, efficient operation. Personnel numbers were relatively the same as the original operation, and the majority of former IFS talents were back, including producer Gregory La Cava, and head of animation, Frank Moser.

Frederick Opper co-writer Louis De Lorme continued scripting *Happy Hooligan*, with cartoonist Walter Lantz replacing Jack King as the new illustrator of the series. King and Bert Gillett were assigned to the new series, *Judge Rummy (Rumhauser)*, based on cartoonist Tad Dorgan's popular comic strip. Bert Green was assigned to illustrate the Dorgan's other new series, *Silk Hat Harry*, about a soda fountain business proprietor. *Krazy Kat* and *Jerry on the Job* were resurrected, and a *Katzenjammer Kids* knock-off, *The Shenanigan Kids*, put into production, animated by Bert Gillett.

Distribution was reestablished with Educational Films Corporation of America, with an official announcement issued by company president Earle W. Hammons. The February 22 issue of *Motion Picture News* reported the agreement, signed earlier in the month, that called for EFC to be the domestic and worldwide distributor of all animated Hearst cartoons.

The article recognized that IFS general manager Carl E. Zittel's attempts to create a Hearst film exchange for distribution of the cartoons had been unsuccessful.

"Mr. Zittel confided in me that for a long time he investigated the dis-

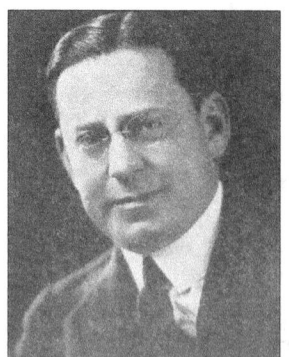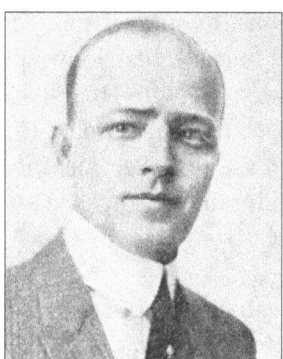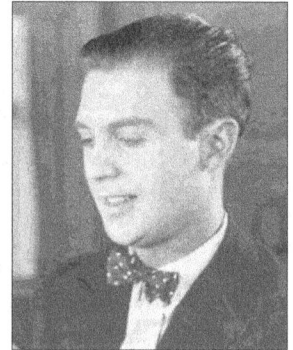

Left to right, EFC president, Earle H. Hammons, IFS manager Carl E. Zittle, and artist Walter Lantz.

tributing end of the business in an effort to find the best distributing facilities," Hammons told *Motion Picture News*. "When he finally decided to let Educational Films Corporation handle the cartoons, he agreed, saying it was 'the best medium' for his product."

After the association, the cartoons went under the brand Hearst-International Cartoons. They were also referred to as International Black and White Comedies. But generally, the business was still identified as International Film Service again.

The road to reestablish IFS had been difficult for Zittel, who endured additional hardship the end of February when his only son, Carl Jr., died from complications resulting from a tonsillectomy. The boy was barely 19.

Educational put the last *Happy Hooligan* cartoon produced, *Smash-Up in China*, back into circulation. By March 1st, the distributor was taking out full-page ads in entertainment and trade magazines, announcing in bold headlines the Hearst cartoons were, "Back Again and Funnier than Ever!"

The first *Happy Hooligan* cartoon produced the new year, *Where Are the Papers?*, was released on March 31. The 28th episode in the series, it enjoyed a private exhibition for the media on February 15.

In the film, Happy Hooligan is entrusted with delivering some important papers to General Pershing. The tramp uses a boat at one point, and endures an amusing encounter with a pelican, who picks him up and carries him away. The tramp's return to theaters was a resounding public success.

On April 5, *Motion Picture News* reported that the arrangement between Hearst animated productions and Educational Films Corporation was already paying off.

"According to officials of Educational Films Corporation of America, the new International Comedies in Black and White, featuring the well-known *Judge Rumhauser*, *The Shenanigan Kids*, and *Happy Hooligan*, have broken all records and approval in the best theaters," the magazine reported.

Earle W. Hammons explained that theaters had "discriminated against 'jerky' cartoons," and found International's "process of double animation more realistic and life-like." He added audiences enjoyed the comedy and smooth action of the Hearst productions.

The next *Happy Hooligan* cartoon, *Knocking the H Out of Heinie*, released April 28, was another patriotic, tall tale of wartime. In the tale, Happy tells his nephews about his bravery and heroics standing guard

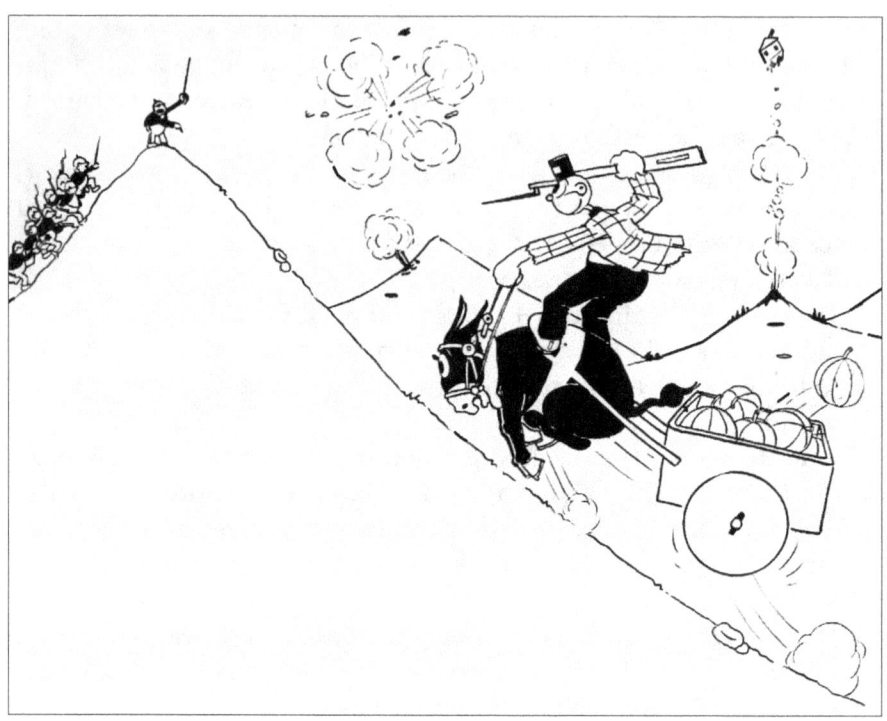

Illustration from the *Happy Hooligan* cartoon *Knocking the H Out of Heinie*, April 28, 1919.

in a battlefront observation tower, with shells whizzing overhead. Riding a donkey drawn cart full of pumpkins and a bayonet in hand, the tramp takes the battle to the enemy, high on a hilltop. For his bravery, a medal is pinned on the victorious Hooligan.

The general public was provided a look inside Hearst's animation studio via a *Motion Picture Magazine* article written by IFS artist, Bert Green. Published in its' May issue, the illustrator of the *Silk Hat Harry* series explained the type and amount of work that went into creating an animated cartoon.

"The process involved is so complicated that it is difficult to explain intelligently because of the great number of parts to a 'subject.' By this I mean the drawings, celluloid, tones, cut-outs, etc., and their relation to one another in order to complete a certain scene," Green said. "It must be borne in mind that film passes thru the projector (of your pet theater) at one foot a second."

Green explained the typical length of animated shorts he worked on for IFS was "fifty to one hundred and fifty feet," for "two minutes and five seconds." That translated into "two thousand individual pictures."

Green said he had two days, to one week to draw a film, and that editors needed to "get over" the idea of being as elaborate as possible.

"The amount of tracing and camera work consumes all kinds of time," Green said. "I have reached a point by experience that if I figure a cartoon needs to be finished and under the camera by five o'clock, I am safe by just adding three more hours for luck."

Green conveyed his experience illustrating a recent episode of the *Silk Hat Harry* cartoon, *Breath of a Nation*, released June 29, involved pictures of a man on the street running back and forth to saloons. Finding all establishments closed, the gentleman drinks from a water spigot.

"I roughly figured I would have to make about one hundred and sixty drawings of the man as he came down the street," Green explained. "But before I had him up to the water faucet I had made about four hundred and fifteen drawings."

Green addressed the grueling schedule at IFS that left little time for anything else.

"It's no use making any engagements while in this business, as you might as well be serving a sentence in Joliet," he said. "I think that if an animated cartoonist had any time to himself he would go to pieces."

Green explained the short amount of time allowed to create a cartoon involved a great number of people, and expense.

"Cartoons like the *Katzenjammer Kids* [former IFS production], *Hap-*

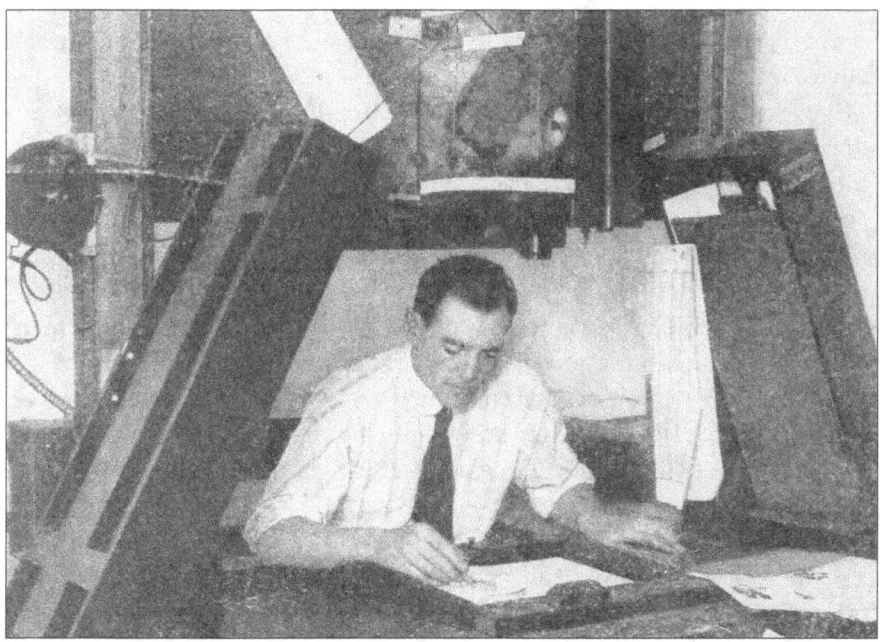

Bert Green in the International Film Service camera room.

py Hooligan, Mutt and Jeff [Fox Film production], etc., that run five hundred feet, require a staff of from fifteen to thirty people, men and women, to produce this amount of animated cartoon a week. With salaries ranging from ten to three hundred dollars per week, you can readily get some idea of the time and expense involved," Green said. "Cartoons such as these contain from two thousand to three thousand drawings, and it takes two photographers one solid week working into nights, under pressure, to photograph these drawings."

Green pointed to IFS animator Frank Moser as being one of the most efficient in the business

"The most rapid animator in the game is Frank Moser. Moser literally shakes them out of a hat," he said. "I have seen Moser take a scenario of *Happy Hooligan* and in thirty days hand you a pile of between two and three thousand drawings that you couldn't jump over and live through it."

Green also explained the complexity of the animation process.

"An animated cartoon is photographed by 'stop motion,' by which we mean one picture to one revolution of the crank instead of sixteen pictures, as is used exclusively in photoplay," he wrote. "This is one reason that makes it a time consumer. Nearly all 'trick photography' is done by 'stop motion.' Unfortunately, I am a glutton for hard work and long hours."

Green concluded the piece with a list of basic requirements, and some advice to prospective animation cartoonists.

"An animated cartoonist must be able to talk English, Irish and Swedish, must know the Ten Commandments, the law of gravitation, locomotion and its uses, mind over matter, psychology and its action on cheese, the rules of the road, 'cohesion' and its lifting capacity, navigation, a strong believer in Darwin, the art of tuning a bass violin, the internal combustion engine and its use in the home, how to fry an egg, many innumerable things touched upon so lightly by our famous men and, above all, the animated cartoonist must have a one-track mind."

The next *Happy Hooligan* cartoon, *Der Wash on Der Line*, was released May 17. In the story, Happy tells his nephews another tall tale, this time how he defeated a large number of Germans during the war.

Entertainment magazines noted the cartoon was "well drawn," and that it offered typical Hooligan "foolishness."

"The film gets pretty near vulgarity in a few places," *Motion Picture News* reported on May 31. "But, on the whole, calls for laughs accompanied by blushes."

In mid-May, Carl E. Zittel issued a statement that International Film Service was now back in the game. *Motion Picture News* published the announcement on May 24.

"In a statement this week General Manager C. F. Zittel, of the International Films Service, announces the plans that have been made, and the work accomplished, in connection with the new series of International cartoon comedies, now being released through the Educational Films Corporation of America," the magazine reported.

Zittel spoke of the challenges of managing an animation studio and the measure of quality it took to create a good cartoon.

"The difficulty of turning out a five-hundred foot cartoon subject is little appreciated by the average exhibitor," he said. "The International studio staff, [is] under the direction of Gregory La Cava, and consists of thirty artists. Finding just the right sort of people for this exacting work is not the least of the difficulties connected with cartoon making. They must be able to appreciate a funny situation from a description, and to bring out all the laughs in their finished drawings. In cartoon work, every line in the sketch, and every second of running time, is a vital part of the finished comedy, and must have the very best attention."

Zittel explained one staffer worked days to produce "a few feet of film," and employees had to maintain a schedule of one subject, or 500 feet, per week. He then outlined the 1918 collapse of IFS, and the reason behind it.

"The old International staff, that produced the original series of twenty-two releases, was thoroughly demoralized by the influenza and the demands for military service last fall, and production had to be stopped," he said. "Now, after months of effort, the staff has been built up again to a point where the quality is assured."

Zittel called the IFS "double animation" process "exclusive," and offered why their studio produced the most enjoyable cartoons.

"This process has been so perfected that the action is as smooth, and natural, as it would be with living characters," he said. "The only noticeable difference being that the comic folk can do stunts that are quite impossible, and therefore funny. Directors take their work seriously. He writes his scenarios, chooses his casts, and arranges the scenes exactly as if the comic folk were real."

Zittel boasted that the reunion with Educational Films Corporation of America allowed for distribution through the sixteen exchanges, resulting in "an almost complete" circulation to the better theatres of this country. The new distribution arrangement also placed the cartoons in foreign markets for the first time.

"The cartoons are being shipped regularly to every foreign sales territory on a contract basis that insures the IFS [overseas] circulation of every release," he said.

Zittel stated new bookings were being, "received daily since the inauguration of the new series in March." He also said communication was established directly with exhibitors to gauge how new product was received, and to entertain suggestions resulting in better comedies.

"Mr. Zittel intends to hold the International comedies in the first rank of cartoon releases—a position which they have earned by past performances," *Motion Picture News* reported. "One little detail of present productions is directors will try to work into each comic reel one funny climax that will be remembered."

The idea was to produce a memorable moment patrons would repeat to their friends. This included the shenanigans of Frederick Opper's character *Happy Hooligan*.

The next *Happy Hooligan* cartoon, *Bringing Home the Bacon*, was released on May 26. The story has Happy Hooligan, with the help of his nephews, scouring the classified newspaper ads to find the hobo a job. But, bringing home the bacon ends up meaning being paired with a pig.

Happy Hooligan in *The Tale of A Shirt*, released on June 9, begins with Happy's nephews shooting at bees. Their uncle tells them to always be kind to creatures, and spins a tale about his experience with the Official Cootie Hound and the cooties. The tale, more like a nightmare, has the hounds reminding Happy he has a wife and five kids. A night scene

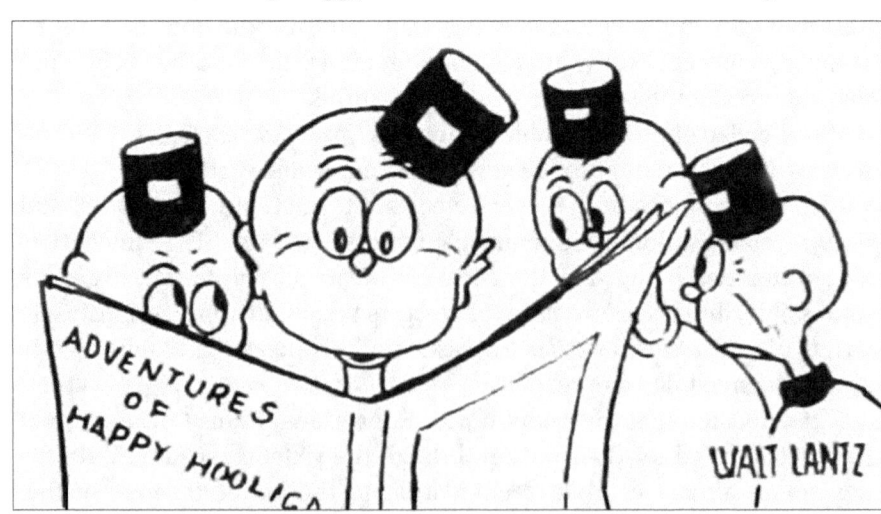

Illustration from the *Happy Hooligan* cartoon *Bringing Home the Bacon*, released May 26, 1919.

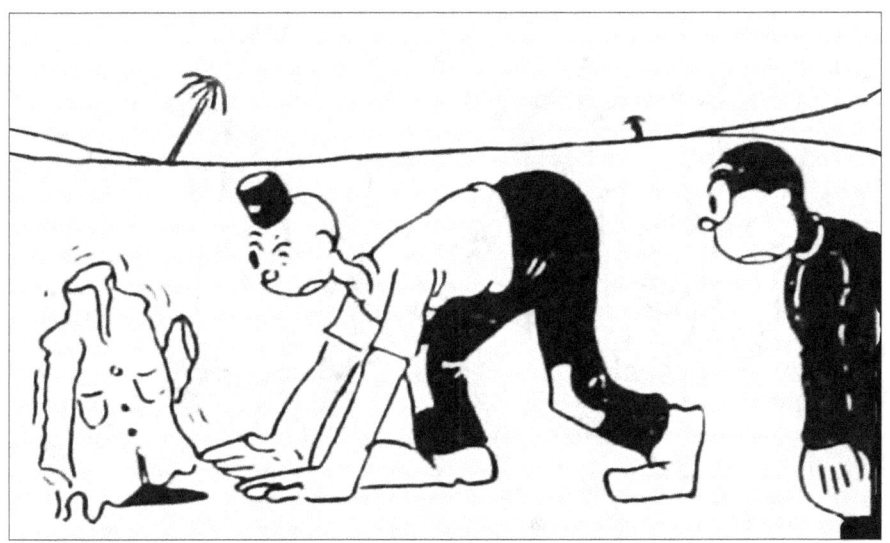

Illustration from the *Happy Hooligan* cartoon *The Tale of a Shirt,* released June 9, 1919.

displays the black sky crumbling, falling to Earth like rubble. The cooties use a searchlight to find, and save, the tramp. The cartoon concludes with Happy being stung by a bee.

"Laughs develop into roars with *Happy Hooligan* in *The Tale of a Shirt,*" *Motion Picture News* reported on June 21.

The following *Happy Hooligan* cartoon, *A Wee Bit 'O Scotch*, released on June 23, places the tramp back on the battlefield. Happy faces off with the Germans, who fire upon him using a cannon. The hobo re-

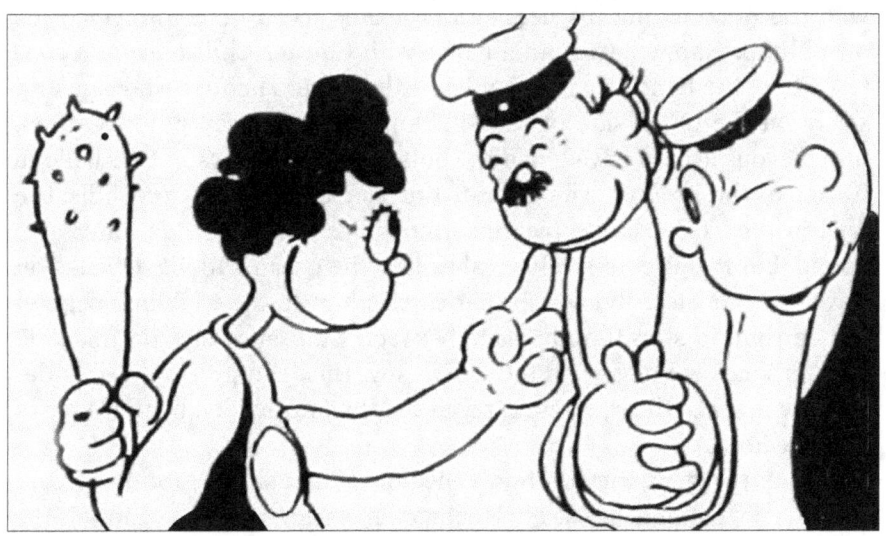

Illustration from the *Happy Hooligan* cartoon *A Wee Bit 'O Scotch,* released June 23, 1919.

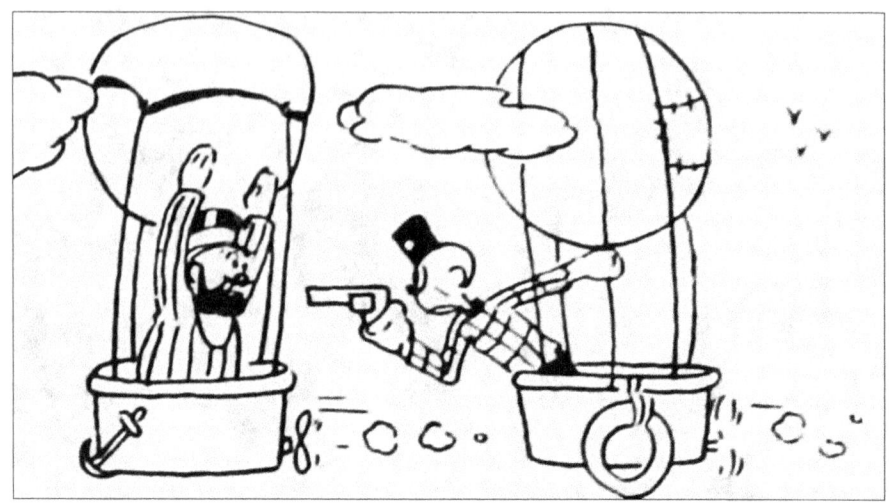

Illustration from the *Happy Hooligan* cartoon *The Perils of Paprika,* released July 7, 1919.

quests a blast-proof outfit, which he calls a "shock proof uniform." Clad in invincible attire, Hooligan easily claims victory.

"There are all sorts of effects used with a comedy touch," *Motion Picture News* reported on July 5.

The Film Daily praised the cartoon.

"A funny subject that is sure of getting laughs is *Happy Hooligan's A Wee Bit of Scotch,*" the *Daily* reported on June 29. "It treats of war in a mighty amusing manner."

Happy Hooligan in *The Perils of Paprika*, released on July 7, begins with the hobo telling his nephews of a time when he commanded his own blimp. Happy enters an air race with Chester Chilisauce in a contest where the hand of a fair maiden is the prize. The first who can land safely on the other side of the kingdom, wins. However, for starters, mischievous agents have glued the bottom of Hooligan's hot air balloon basket to the ground. The aircraft breaks free, and he and Chilisauce duel in the sky. A bullet piercing Hooligan's balloon sends him Earth bound, but the airship safely crashes into the ocean. Hooligan walks on waves and meets a flying fish that carries him to the wedding location just in time to stop the marriage between Chilisauce and the maiden. The "groom" is exposed as a German spy, thus Happy Hooligan is declared winner of the race. He is rewarded the fair maiden by the Duke of Muttonchops.

"An extravagant cartoon and ridiculously amusing," *Motion Picture News* reported on August 2. "Hooligan is getting where he can tell the biggest whoppers. It's a side splitting cartoon."

Happy Hooligan in *A Jungle Jumble*, released on July 21, depicted African-Americans in a shockingly stereotypical manner. A hefty-sized "mammy" maid appears, as well as a jaunt back to Africa for some tribal comparisons. Apparently, leading entertainment magazines shied away from the cartoon, and didn't review it.

The next *Happy Hooligan* cartoon, *Turkey Hash*, released August 10, isn't about Thanksgiving dinner. In the story, Happy spins a tale that places him in the nation of Turkey, where he is an ambassador. The hobo gets into an international fix when he heroically enters a sultan's harem to rescue the fair maidens.

Happy Hooligan in *The Great Handicap*, released on August 24, places the hobo in a great automobile race, in which he is the victor. The film is an example of some of the earliest animated shorts that featured automobile racing as a sport. But, Happy's nephews don't believe this latest tall tale.

"The Great Handicap compares well in quality to recent releases," *Wid's Film Daily* noted. "There is a full quota of the sort of humor found in these subjects in the film."

The following *Happy Hooligan* cartoon, *After the Ball*, released on September 28, has Uncle Happy telling his nephews another major league exaggeration, this one with their hobo uncle at bat on a baseball field. But not in a major league game, a little league one, with the boy hobo outplaying every other kid on the diamond.

In the next *Happy Hooligan* cartoon, *Business is Business*, released

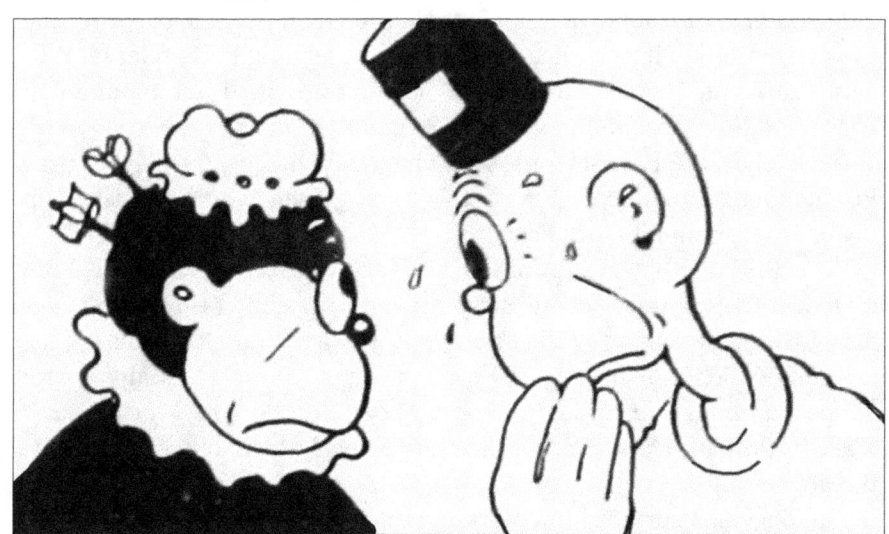

Illustration from the *Happy Hooligan* cartoon *A Jungle Jumble,* released July 21, 1919.

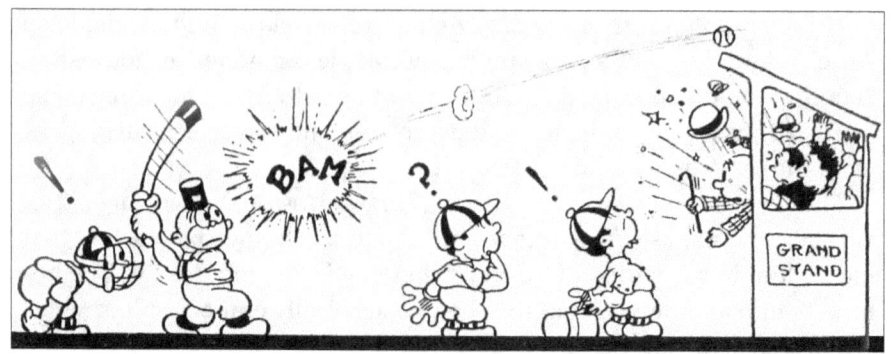

Illustration from the *Happy Hooligan* cartoon *After the Ball*, released September 28, 1919.

on November 23, Happy tells his nephews that minding one's business is always the best policy. The tale unfolds into a litany of examples where curiosity, or trying to help others, can lead one into a mess. The most prominent segment features Happy as "a great detective" who is sent out to quiet two parties engaged in a battle royale. Happy is about to arrest one of the men, who appears to be beating his wife, when he discovers they are all actors performing in a play. At the conclusion, Happy asks his nephews to break the rule of not getting involved when he is swept into a coal shoot and requires rescue.

"The cartoon is below the standard usually maintained," *Wid's Film Daily* stated. "It includes several bits that have no real connection with the main theme and that in itself lacks novelty and quality. But, on the whole, this is a suitable little offering."

Business is Business was the final *Happy Hooligan* release produced by International Film Service. In the months leading to its release, William Randolph Hearst had entered negotiations with John Randolph Bray to take over production of all IFS animated series.

In October, the Hearst comic strip characters had been leased to Bray Productions. Announcements of this arrangement were published in major entertainment periodicals.

"The Bray Pictures Corporation has secured the International Film cartoons, the originals [comic strip versions] appear in the Hearst syndicate of newspapers," *Wid's Film Daily* reported on October 21. "The cartoons which will now be released through [Samuel] Goldwyn are: *Judge Rumhauser, Happy Hooligan, Krazy Kat, Jerry on the Job* and *The Shenanigan Kids*. The series were formerly distributed by Educational."

Full page ads surfaced in entertainment and trade magazines on November 1, promoting the IFS cartoon lineup coming from Bray Productions. The cartoons would be released under the "Goldwyn Bray Pictograph" banner.

The November 1 issue of *Motion Picture News* outlined further details of the International Film Service/Bray Productions association.

"*Judge Rumhauser, Happy Hooligan, Krazy Kat, Jerry on the Job*, the *Shenanigan Kids*, all famous characters that appear in the Hearst

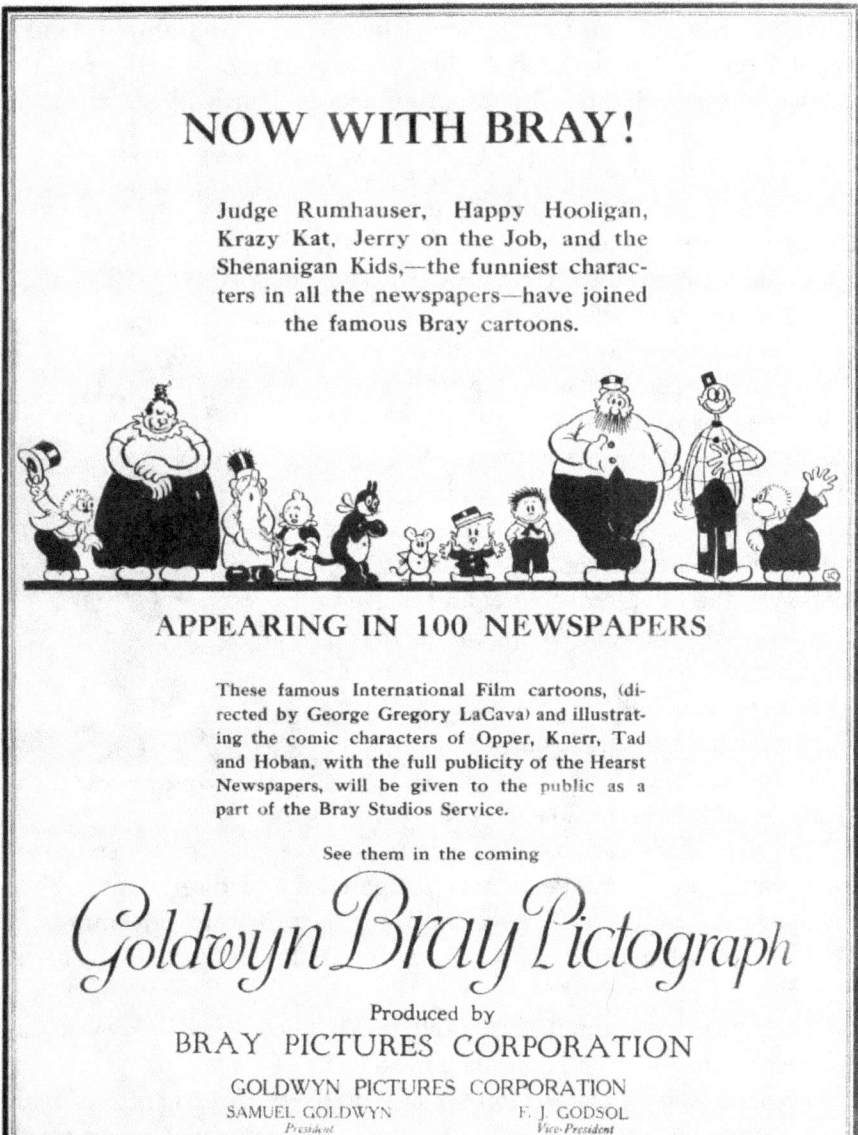

Goldwyn Bray Pictograph advertisement announcing the IFS line-up, fall 1919.

newspapers throughout the country, are moving to the Bray Studios to ally themselves with J. R. Bray's comedy creations," the magazine reported. "Through a deal consummated last week between Bray Pictures Corporation and the International Film Company, the screen versions of the popular newspaper personalities in the Hearst family will hereafter reach the public via Goldwyn-Bray Pictographs, joining the other Bray releases."

According to *Motion Picture News*, the alliance gave Goldwyn "a monopoly" on the "most widely known comedy cartoon creations in the country." It also elevated Bray to prominence as the leading animation producer in America.

"The cartoons made at the Bray Studios and those of the International Film Service, the cartoon department of which is headed by George Gregory La Cava, are without question the most popular of all the funny little black and white people who come to life on the screens of motion picture theatres," the magazine stated. "Millions of people now follow the antics of these interesting products from the brains of ingenious comic artists. When it was first attempted to give animation to the pen and ink drawings, the motion of the figures was jerky and uneven, but hundreds of experiments conducted in the Bray Studios have resulted in a process that gives absolute smoothness and lifelikeness to the odd little characters."

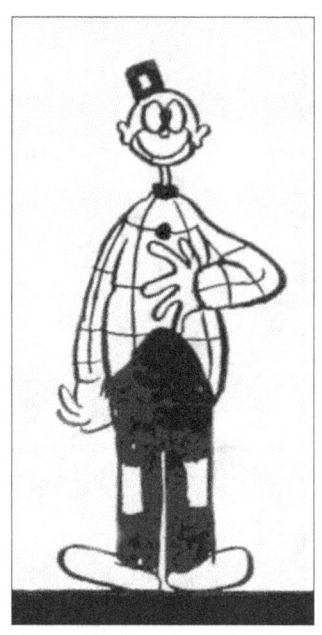

Happy Hooligan, headed to Bray Productions.

Which matched the quality standards Hearst's animation studio had produced.

"The Bray Corporation will continue to make all of its series of cartoons which for several years have delighted the picture-going public," the magazine reported. "These include the humorous adventures of *Colonel Heeza Liar*, *Dud* and *Us Fellers*, and the *Out of the Inkwell* creations by Max Fleischer."

The report also noted that Bray, in alliance with Goldwyn, was "perfecting the world's first cartoon in color."

The other side of the dealmaker coin that was Bray had previously been distributed by Paramount, and now, after securing Goldwyn with an agreement, the animation studio would expand. According to *Motion*

Picture News, the acquisition of IFS content placed him "in accord with his policy of expansion following the alliance with Goldwyn."

The official IFS arrangement with Bray would be initiated at the beginning of 1920. IFS would continue producing the cartoons from their studio, but mainly focus on feature film projects.

By the year's end, Carl E. Zittel quit the Heart's animation branch. In fact, Zittel resigned twice. Once in November. He reconsidered, returned, then turned in a second resignation effective December 1.

The announcement published in *The Exhibitor's Herald*, stated that Zittel, "could not deal with increasing demands of International." departure merely meant he would focus his time on the motion picture department of Hearst's *New York Journal* and *New York American* newspapers. He would also look after the affairs of the Campbell Studio.

It was more a fanciful way of saying that Zittel was merely being directed elsewhere in the Hearst film organization.

Frederick Opper continued to see his character's popularity increase. The *Happy Hooligan* comics page for Hearst newspapers was one of the most highly rated comics among readers in 1919.

The year 1920 saw the return of *Happy Hooligan*, this time under the Bray Productions banner. However, problems would surface early on. In a little more than two years *Happy Hooligan* would vanish from the world of animation.

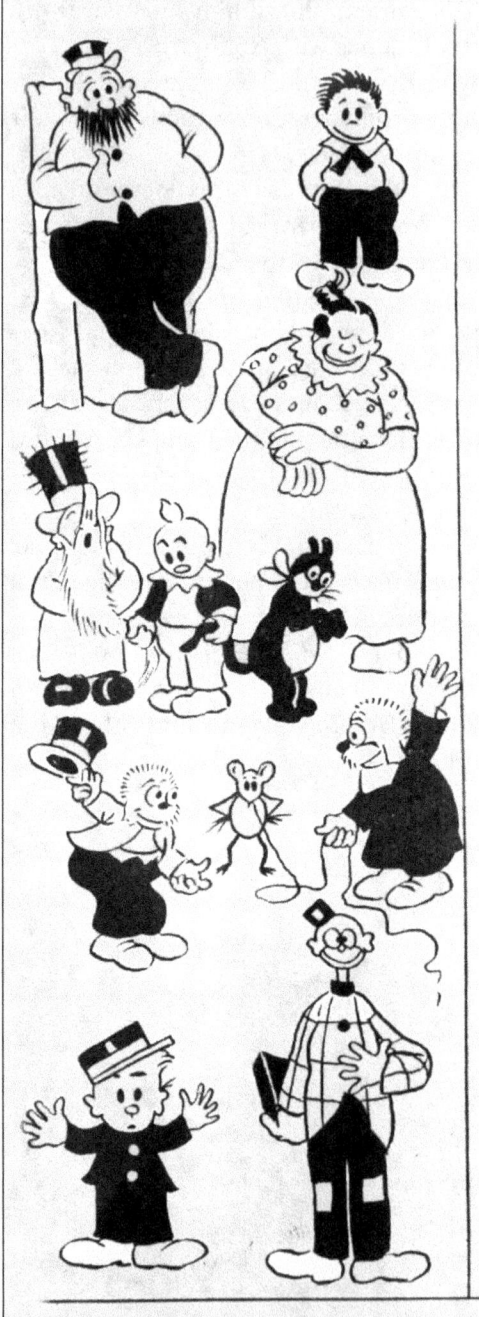

The Maximum of Entertainment

Goldwyn-Bray releases are the concentrated essence of entertainment. Only subjects of vital interest to the public are selected. All corners of the world are portrayed with a twist of novelty which is peculiarly BRAY — absorbing educationals, always of timely interest.

Bray animated cartoons bring roars of laughter. The funniest of all cartoon characters— Jerry on the Job, Happy Hooligan, Shenanigan Kids, Silk Hat Harry and Krazy Kat—

APPEARING DAILY IN OVER 100 NEWSPAPERS,

have joined the Bray forces.

These famous international black and white comedies, illustrating the comic characters of Opper, Knerr, Tad and Hoban, with the full publicity of the Hearst newspapers, are given to the public in the Bray studios releases.

Every subject short, crisp and concise — the maximum of entertainment in the minimum of footage.

Goldwyn Bray Releases

Produced by
BRAY PICTURES CORP.

GOLDWYN PICTVRES CORPORATION

SAMVEL GOLDWYN Presid

Advertisement announcing the Goldwyn-Bray line-up of film cartoons, 1920.

CHAPTER EIGHT
Bray's Hooligan Cartoons 1920-22

The year 1920 began with the International Film Service cartoon characters in production under the Goldwyn-Bray arrangement. The direction was to issue a weekly *Goldwyn-Bray Comic*, a single reel subject distributed weekly beginning April 18. They would also release a new split-reel comedy cartoon featuring the IFS favorites in the first half, and an unrelated, but animated, "lampoon" tackling current topics.

"It will be unlike anything heretofore presented on the screen," the April 10 issue of *The Moving Picture World* reported. "It is enlisting the services of the foremost cartoonists and humorists of the country." The first half of the film reintroduced the IFS cartoon characters *Happy Hooligan*, *The Shenanigan Kids* with *The Captain and The Inspector*, *Judge Rumhauser*, and *Silk Hat Harry*.

"All of these characters are known to hundreds of thousands of newspaper readers, and their humor is more contagious than ever when conveyed through the black and white figures on the silver screen," *The Moving Picture World* added.

With the number of series came the IFS staff that worked on them, as part of Bray's expansion promise to Goldwyn. But, at least initially, the employees operated from the IFS studio. Gregory La Cava, John Foster, William Nolan, Vernon Stallings, Ben Sharpsteen, and Walter Lantz were among the familiar faces that now produced content for Goldwyn-Bray under a lease agreement.

"The Bray Pictures Corporation believes it is fortunate in securing the exclusive marketing rights to International cartoon productions," the magazine said. "The popularity of these funny characters, combined

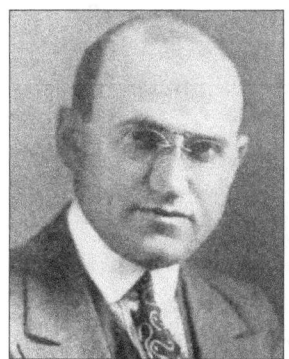 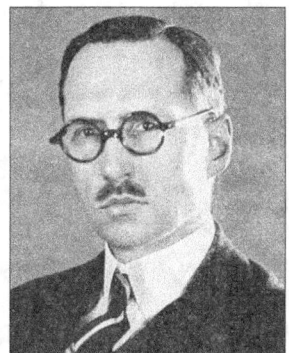 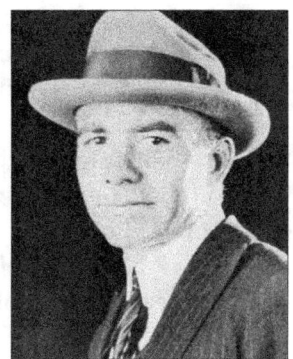

Left to right, Samuel Goldwyn, John Randolph Bray, and Gregory La Cava.

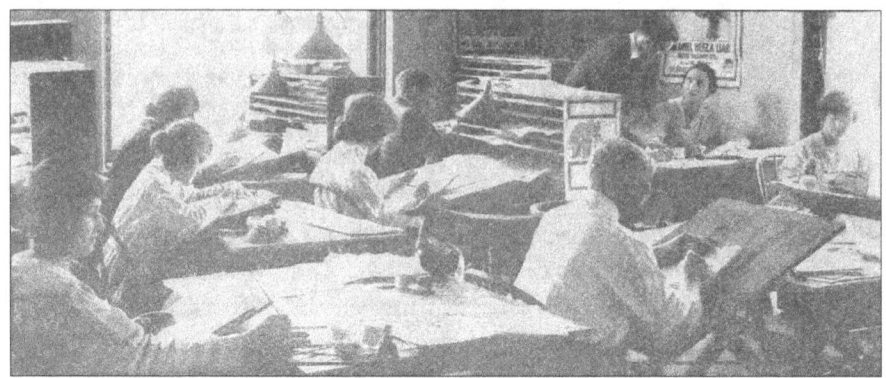

Employees working in a corner of the Bray Studio art department, 1917.

with the long experience and technical skill of the two staffs, insures releases which are even superior to past pictures in the series."

Frederick Opper's partner in plots, story writer Louis De Lorme, wrote the series until the end of the year, then departed. Other staff writers would contribute to *Happy Hooligan's* 1921-22 cartoons.

Business Digest and Investment Weekly announced the details of the Goldwyn-Bray partnership on February 10. Goldwyn wasn't merely a distributor, it essentially owned Bray Pictures, via a million-and-a-half dollar takeover.

"The Goldwyn Pictures Corporation announces the purchase of a controlling interest in Bray Pictures Corporation, the leading producer of scenic, comedy, cartoon, educational and industrial picture films," *Business Digest and Investment Weekly* reported. "The new deal promises a vast increase in output, covering all fields in the Bray corporation's interests."

The first Bray *Happy Hooligan* cartoon, *The Great Umbrella Mystery*, was released on April 17. In the story, Happy tries out a scheme to make money by repairing umbrellas. When he is about to give up, in disgust, he discovers a paper outlining the whereabouts of a treasure box. He goes on an adventure in search of the prize, but upon finding it sees the box contains nothing but umbrellas.

"Drawn and animated excellently," *Wid's Daily* reported on April 18. "The *Happy Hooligan* cartoon, which makes up the greater part of this Bray comic, holds its own. The theme is fairly clever, the various bits funny and executed splendidly. The cartoon part [of the reel] will get over with ease in all probability."

Happy Hooligan, in *The First Man to the Moon*, was released April 21. In the story, a professor sends the tramp to the moon riding atop a rocket. Happy crash lands safely on the lunar surface, where he finds a race of one-eyed people who crown him "King of the Moon." The aliens include a creature with a horn for a nose and another with the body of a bird cage. They perform for the hobo. Happy even dances with a ballerina. The tale concludes with Hooligan being awakened on a park bench by a police officer. The story was only a dream.

In *Happy Hooligan, A Fish Story*, released on July 18, the hobo tells his nephews of a successful, but hazardous, fishing expedition. With his boat full of fish, the seas kick up. Happy is helplessly carried about the waves. He is rescued by some kindly fish, who carry him back home. To show his appreciation, the tramp releases all the fish he had caught.

"The *Happy Hooligan* cartoon is similar to most of these, in which the character has been seen," *Wid's Daily* reported on July 25. "A satisfactory idea, executed so as to provoke titters."

The Goldwyn-Bray arrangement was in full production mode, but behind the scenes some tricky business was taking place.

In June, the contract with director William Nolan was not renewed, and Bray owed International Film Service studio $41,000, according to their lease. Hearst had revealed little to Goldwyn at the time of the Bray association that the IFS cartoons were becoming unprofitable.

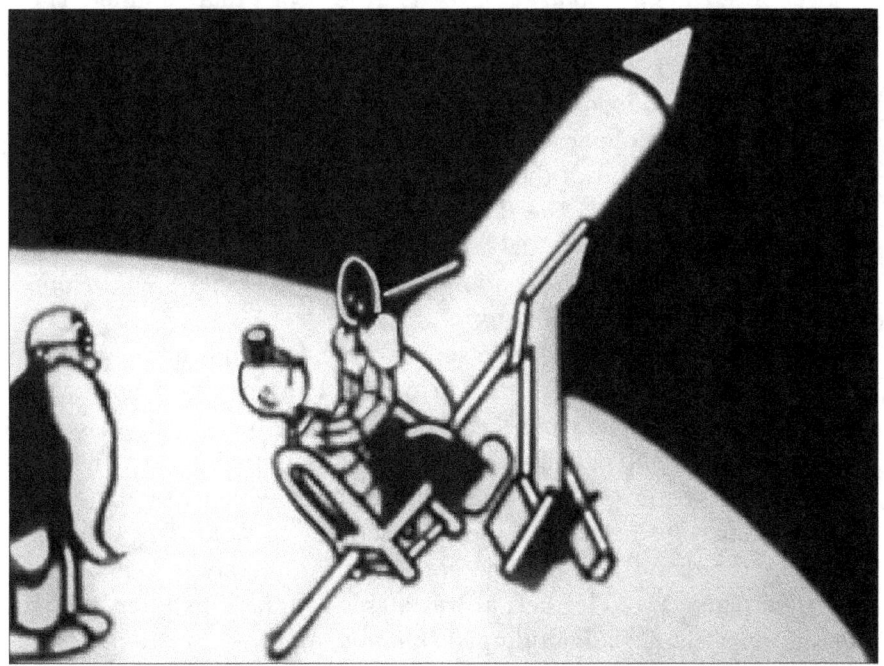

Frame from the *Happy Hooligan* cartoon *First Man to the Moon,* released April 21, 1920.

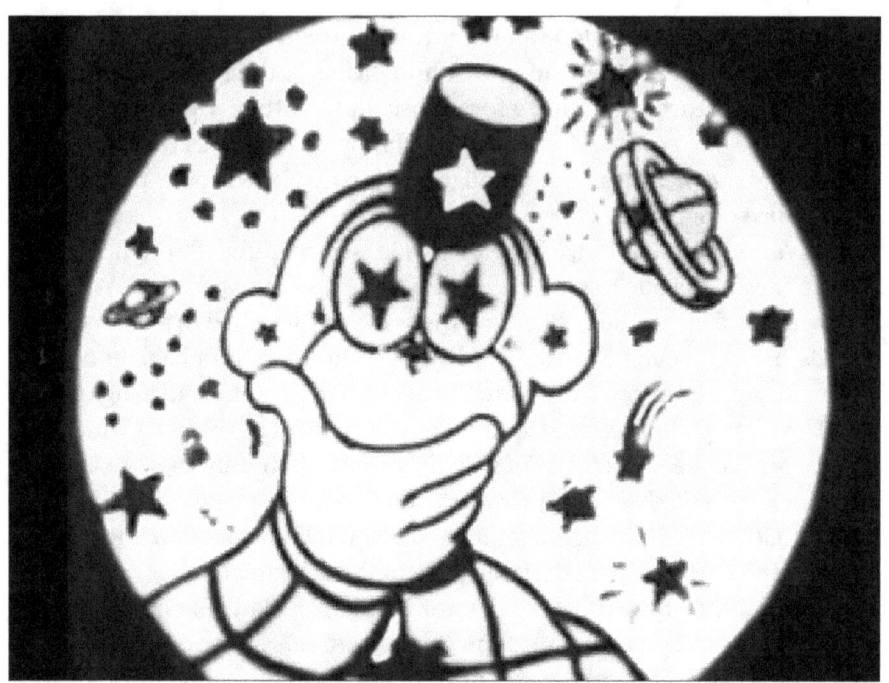
Frame from the *Happy Hooligan* cartoon *First Man to the Moon,* released April 21, 1920.

Five more *Happy Hooligan* cartoons were issued that summer. They included: *The Last Rose of Summer*, released on August 1, *Cupid's Advice*, on August 11, *A Fly Guy*, on August 15, *Happy Hoolidini*, on September 11, and *Apollo*, on September 18. The themes included Happy in love, a Harry Houdini parody, and mixing it up with a Greek god.

From fall to the end of the year, six *Happy Hooligan* cartoons were released. They included: *The Blacksmith*, on October 10, *A Doity Deed*, on October 25, *The Boot Black*, on November 7, *A Romance of '76*, on November 22, *Doctor Jekyll and Mr. Zipp*, on December 8, and *Happy Hooligan In Oil*, on December 23.

With the releases came criticism, and the first indication that the cleverness of stories and animation quality had entered a downward curve. The entertainment press conveyed in many ways, without saying it, that *Happy Hooligan* had outlived his glory days in film cartoons.

The departure in quality likely corresponded with writer Louis De Lorme's departure from the series. In fact, due to Goldwyn's schedule demands and demeanor, history records that "a massive exodus of talent" took place. Max Fleisher, a Bray staple in talent, had departed in June. Gregory La Cava had jumped ship, too, and was directing motion pictures for other filmmakers.

Sometime after this, La Cava reflected on his animation days in an article published in *Motion Picture Classic* magazine. He conveyed that entering animation was only a wedge into a broader range of the film industry. The experience helped him with directing live-action films.

"I can almost always tell how many frames it will take to make a given gesture," he said, due to his experience with cartoons.

Many lawsuits were filed during the two-year Goldwyn, Bray and International Film Service agreement. Suits between IFS and Goldwyn-Bray made headlines. Employees on both sides of the fence also sued for nonpayment or breach of contract.

Vernon Stallings and Walter Lantz stayed on, however, both in acting roles of "co-producers."

Reviews of the *Happy Hooligan* cartoons were less that stellar.

In *A Doity Deed*, Happy must bring home a bride to inherit his father's fortune. After several futile efforts, the tramp gets a widow to consent. The only problem is that the woman is followed by several young-

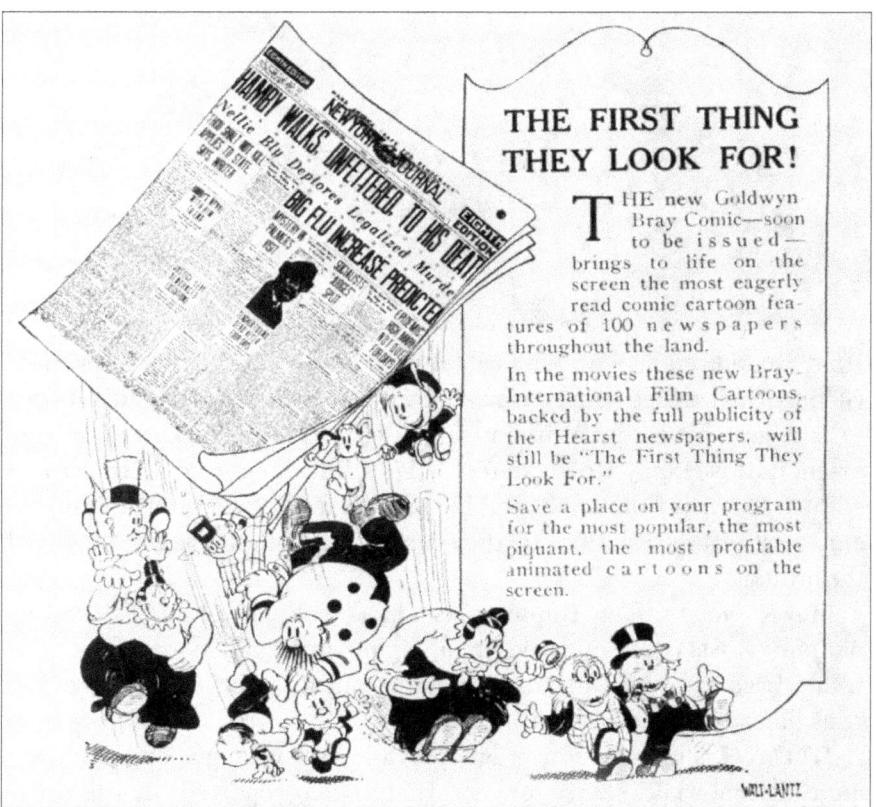

Goldwyn-Bray cartoon advertisement illustrated by Walter Lantz, 1920.

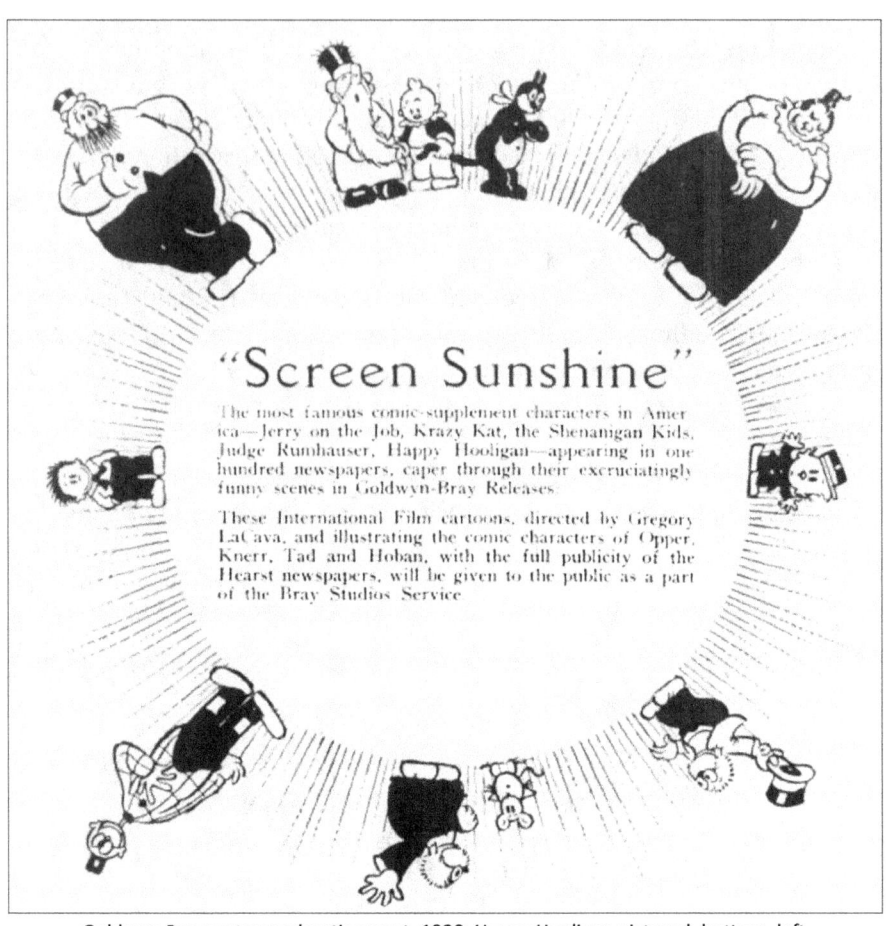

Goldwyn-Bray cartoon advertisement, 1920. Happy Hooligan pictured, bottom, left.

sters. Do kids come with the deal? But no matter, as the hobo's brother, Gloomy Gus, brings home a wax model of a woman and get dad's stash.

"The greatest essential in any animated cartoon is lacking to a large extent in this Happy Hooligan reel," *Wid's Daily* reported in its October edition. "Some of the incidental business is fairly clever, but the theme and most of the situations, if they can be called that, are hardly out of the ordinary."

In *A Romance of '76*, Happy spins a fable that places him back in Revolutionary wartime, engaged in a highly imaginative romance. The tramp tries to elope with a fair maiden, but his brother, Gloomy Gus, wins the lady's hand instead.

"This reel is just about average, providing a few laughs and sufficient amusing material to carry it over," *Wid's Daily* reported. "It will prove satisfactory where a short filler is wanted."

In *Doctor Jekyll and Mr. Zip*, Happy Hooligan appears in a parody of Robert Louis Stevenson's horror classic novel.

By 1921, Goldwyn-Bray was aware that *Happy Hooligan* cartoons were no longer the rave. Thus, only three animated titles featuring the tramp were released that year.

The first *Happy Hooligan* of the new year, *Roll Your Own*, was released on January 3, 1921. In the tale, Happy is in Mexico painting signs and falls in love with a señorita whose father stages bullfights. When a bull set to go in the ring dies, the tramp takes its place by wearing a hide, disguised as a cow. Happy is victorious over the matador he faces and wins the hand of the young lady.

Wid's Daily cut the hobo a break.

"This is the funniest *Happy Hooligan* reel in some time," *Wid's Daily* reported on January 2, 1921. "There are more than the average number of laughs in this one, and this will make a good filler where a cartoon is wanted."

Happy Hooligan, in *Fatherly Love*, was released January 3, 1921. In the tale, Happy and his brother, Gloomy Gus, are aiding and abetting the impending demise of their ailing father, by chilling him when he is cold and roasting him when he is warm. The elder Hooligan finally kicks the bucket. Happy and Gus sell his clothing, then look for the fortune they believe he left behind. The old man's will states that a map to a buried treasure is in one of his old shoes, but the siblings sold the pair. To get them back, Happy plays a cat climbing fences and collects several pairs of old footwear. They recover the map and dig up the trunk, only to discover it contains 400 pairs of old shoes.

Wid's Daily wasn't as kind in their next *Happy Hooligan* review.

"Laughs aren't as numerous in this *Happy Hooligan* cartoon as some proceeding numbers," *Wid's Daily* reported. "There isn't a great deal of amusement, and the reel is below the average *Hooligan* cartoon."

Happy Hooligan, in *A Close Shave*, was released on April 29. But it got lost in promotion due to another short film bearing the same title, in theaters at the same time. It starred Ben Turpin, who was known for playing *Happy Hooligan* in vaudeville.

John R. Bray had mostly lost interest in the animation side of his production company. For some time he had be focusing on establishing a series of live-action comedy shorts to compete with Hal Roach.

The impending animated conclusion of *Happy Hooligan* become relatively clear. Frederick Opper entered an agreement with Gus Hill at the end of 1921 to put the character back into stage productions.

Nearly seven years had passed since Hill had spearheaded a bogus, unauthorized, *Happy Hooligan* movie. William Randolph Hearst had the film pulled out of theaters and destroyed the prints as the result of a judgment. Hearst had represented Opper's interests, also, in the suit.

The old wounds, and perhaps the fading cinematic life of *Happy Hooligan*, made the opportunity look reasonable. The script for the first play, *Down on the Farm*, was written by Richard F. Carroll and John Mulgrew. It was completed in January 1922.

Down on the Farm opened at the Colonial Theater in Utica, New York, in mid-February.

The year 1922 saw the farewell of *Happy Hooligan* in animated cartoons. Only three titles were released that year, the first being *Happy Hooligan* in *The Tale of the Kangaroo*, on March 12. In it, the tramp faces off with a marsupial.

Happy Hooligan, in *Spider and the Fly*, was released on April 9, 1922. It had the hobo in the clouds. Happy doesn't wish to chop wood and is drawn away by a spider who suggests he follow him. The spider spins an enormous web upward to the sky, which the tramp climbs like a rope, reaching the clouds. Once there, Happy discovers a city, and a man, who impresses on him that work is required. The tramp ignores him, and a

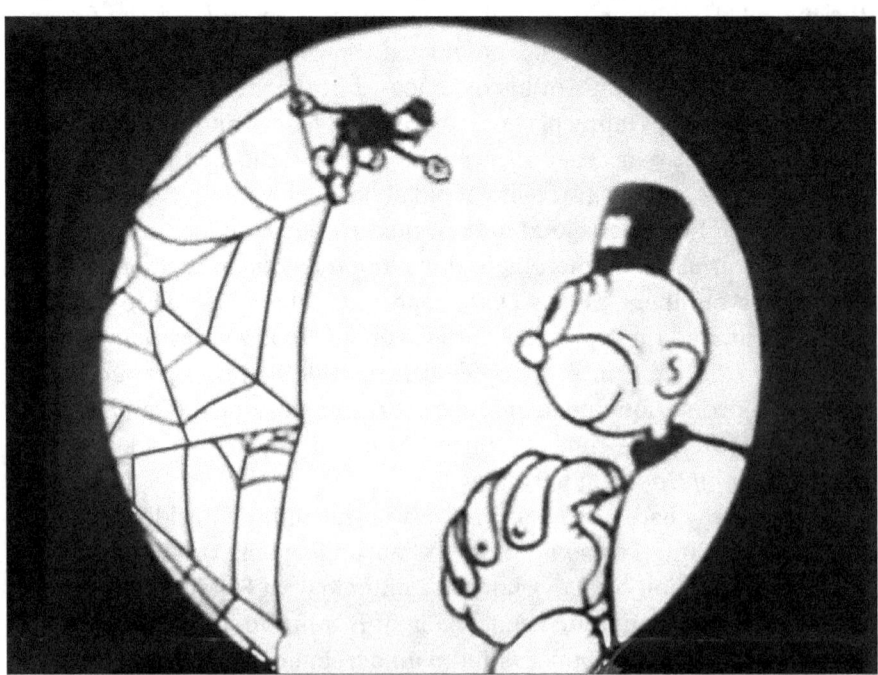

Frame from the *Happy Hooligan* cartoon *Spider and the Fly*, released April 9, 1922.

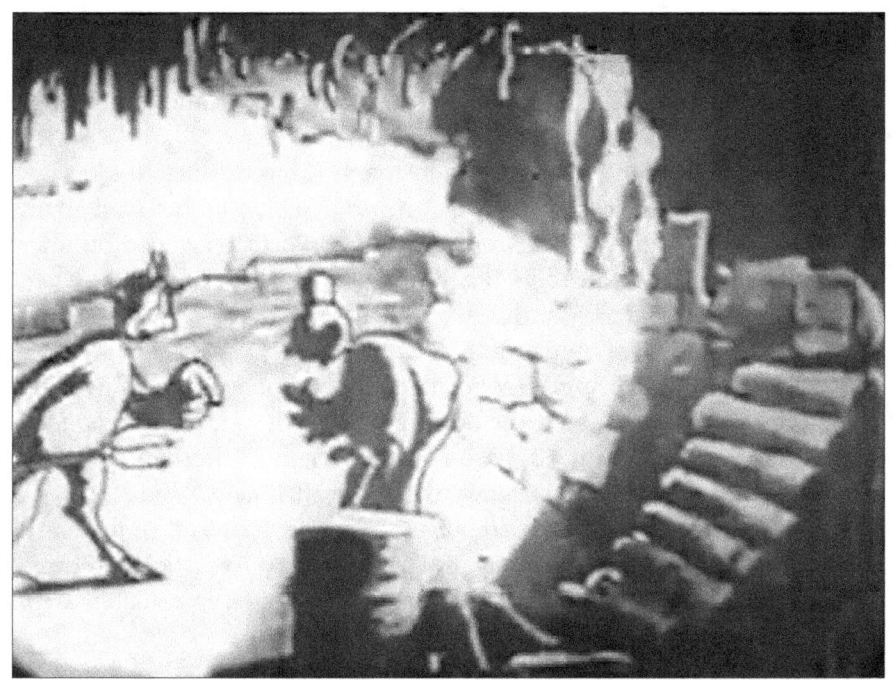
Happy faces off with the Devil in *Spider and the Fly,* released April 9, 1922.

scuffle ensues. Happy is tossed out of the heavenly realm, down through the earth. Emerging in a fiery cave, Happy finds himself in hell, facing the Devil. Work is required there, too, stoking the furnace. But in the end, Happy escapes a very hot situation.

Happy Hooligan, in *Getting the Goods,* was released on April 23, 1922. *Motion Picture News* reported the film rated a 69 out of 100 for entertainment value, and 67 for box office value.

Variety reported in its November 10 edition, "The *Happy Hooligan* comic [cartoon] provided many good laughs."

With the release of *Getting the Goods,* Frederick Opper's *Happy Hooligan* departed the world of animated cartoons. However, the tramp did pop up in one more cartoon, unauthorized, as a parody.

Famous *New York Times* caricature artist, Edwin Marcus, in his *Animated Hair Cartoons* series, episode *KK,* borrowed several of his colleague's creations from the comics' pages for lampoon purposes.

The series, distributed by Red Seal Picture Corporation, was a favorite cartoon oddity with theatergoers.

The characters included in Marcus' parody included *Buster Brown, Happy Hooligan, Mike and Ike* and *Mutt and Jeff.* In the cartoon, one "borrowed" character morphs into the next.

"The transition of *Buster Brown* to *Happy Hooligan* is particularly clever," *Exhibitor's Trade Review* reported on May 16, 1925. "A novelty of this nature should find favor where this sort of entertainment is popular."

"For fun, for which he apologizes to them, [Marcus does this] at the expense of his fellow cartoonists, by drawings which he deftly changes into similar characters," *The Moving Picture World* conveyed on May 16, 1925. "Including Outcault's *Buster Brown*, Opper's *Happy Hooligan*, Goldberg's *Mike and Ike*, and Bud Fisher's *Mutt and Jeff*. This should prove one of the most popular of the *Hair* cartoons."

Frederick Opper's *Happy Hooligan* comics character enjoyed five and a half years as an animated cartoon series. In all, 55 *Happy Hooligan* cartoons had been produced, 37 under the original International Film Service operation, 17 for the Goldwyn-Bray arrangement.

Sadly, only a handful of the *Happy Hooligan* cartoons currently exist. Perhaps this will change, as many of the cartoons were distributed overseas, and in the near future, some century-old, dusty film canisters with be discovered.

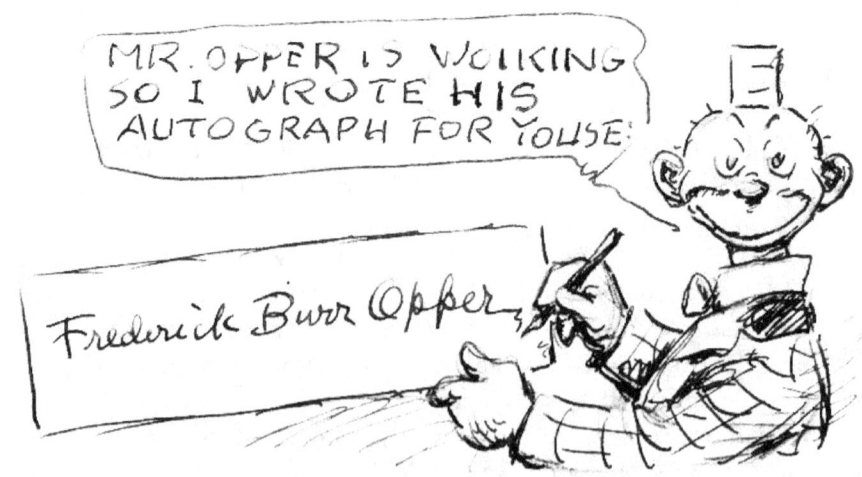